JAPAN: A WORLD PROBLEM

JAPAN:
A WORLD PROBLEM

H. J. Timperley

•

THE JOHN DAY COMPANY
NEW YORK

MANUFACTURED IN THE UNITED STATES OF AMERICA

Contents

Preface

Much of the material used here was gathered in 1935 and 1936 in preparation for a book that was to have called attention to the inevitability of a Sino-Japanese conflict. War broke out before that project could be completed and the work was laid aside. Although the bulk of my notes are now in Japanese hands, I have felt it timely to attempt a reconstruction of my thesis in the light of recent events and with the object of presenting the problem of Japan in what I feel to be its true perspective.

My view of the matter is that, stripped down to its fundamentals, the quarrel between Japan, as at present constituted, and ourselves is simply, in the words of the late Lord Salisbury, "that perpetual form of quarrel which, in its nature, is irreconcilable, and which must always exist between those who wish to conquer and those who desire not to be conquered—between those who mean to eat and those who are averse to being eaten." I believe that too much attention has been paid to the supposed economic causes of the conflict and too little to those deep-rooted psychological forces that have been spurring on the Japanese to world domination. History demonstrates that megalomaniacal ideas have been working in the blood of the Japanese, not merely for generations but for centuries, and that the minds of the Japanese people have been deliberately warped by their military masters. Obviously there can be no durable peace in the Far East, or for that matter in the world at large, until the power of the military oligarchy that now runs Japan has been finally broken.

Just how that is to be achieved I do not pretend to know. Postulating an anti-Axis victory, it should be possible to disarm Japan in a material sense; her psychological disarmament will be much more difficult. All I have sought to do here is to state the problem which Japanese militarism constitutes for the democratic section of the world. It is a problem that is precisely similar, in many respects, to that presented to us by Nazi Germany. In both cases we are faced with nations who are wedded to the principle that the individual is nothing and the State everything, and who are determined to enforce acceptance of this doctrine upon the rest of the world.

To some it may seem premature to go into the question of postwar settlements, as I have done in my Conclusion, at a time when it is quite impossible to predict the military, political and psychological situation at the close of hostilities which have only just begun to reach their full force and tempo. I believe with Walter Lippmann in the importance of getting it firmly fixed in our minds now, however, that postwar planning is not to be regarded as something apart from the war effort but as a means of consolidating the gains, in terms of human happiness and freedom, which we hope that effort will eventually win.

I wish to express here my indebtedness to the many

friends who have helped me with constructive criticism of the book in various stages of preparation—particularly Dr. M. S. Bates and Mr. Harry B. Price, for whose advice and encouragement I am deeply grateful.

In view of my present connection with the National Government of China I deem it advisable to state that the views set forth in this volume are entirely personal and unofficial.

H. J. TIMPERLEY.

New York City,
February 15, 1942.

JAPAN:
A WORLD PROBLEM

I

Background of *Bushido*

"THE history of Japan," it has been said, "is ten centuries of legend, seven centuries of copying and uncopying the Chinese, eight centuries of feudalism, and something over half of one century of capitalism." This simplification throws into relief the brevity of Japan's modern era against the historical background from which it has emerged.

From Old Japan come influences that have profoundly affected the course of the country's subsequent development and are still potent today. They enter into the character of her people and the form of her institutions. Without some reference to them there can be no real understanding of the pace at which Japan has modernized, the swiftness with which she has risen to power, or the momentum behind an expansionist program which today challenges at once the independence of China and the security of Western nations.

FEUDALISTIC FETTERS

When, during the centuries before Christ, successive waves of venturesome immigrants from Manchuria,

Korea, Malaysia, and to a lesser extent China, made their way across the sea to a group of islands now known as Honshu, Kyushu, Shikoku and Hokkaido, they found considerable numbers of aborigines already in possession. These inhabitants resented the encroachment and contested fiercely every foot gained by the intruders. The violent struggle continued intermittently for centuries. Gradually the continentals pushed back the native inhabitants and won control over most of the islands.

Subsequently there developed in Japan among these settlers a patriarchal or clan society. As strong families increased their control over land and built up their fighting resources, a feudal culture slowly emerged. Great military feudal lords known as *daimyo* became the dominant figures in the social order. Japan's long feudal history bristles with exciting stories of struggles between rival *daimyo* for predominance. A group of them ultimately became powerful enough to seize political power, and they fastened upon the country a government based on feudal regulation. Thus reinforced, feudalism persisted until after the middle of the nineteenth century. To some extent it is to be found in Japan even today.

"The continued extension of the old feudal status after the passing of the feudal regime," wrote Hiro-o Sassa, a well-known Japanese journalist, in *Contemporary Japan* in 1937, "is clearly illustrated by the development of both the political parties and the capitalists through compromises made with the clan forces, which preserve the substance and traditions of feudalism. It is also reflected in the country's land and tenant systems, and these in turn are still exerting their effect upon laborers' wages as well as upon the labor union system in manufacturing centers. In effect, the whole economic machinery is influenced by feudal tradition. . . ."

"The integrating traditions of feudalism have not only survived in the strong element of government control and direction of the national economy, but have also survived in the system of national education. . . . In summary, it can be said that Japanese public opinion owes its present nature to feudal conditions, Buddhist and Shinto influences and the family system, together with the survival of all these in the modern development of administration, economic organization and the system of education." [1]

THE SWORD OF THE SAMURAI

For their controversies with rival lords the *daimyo* early recruited and nurtured a hereditary class of professional warriors called *samurai* to whom they accorded the highest social status. Next in the social scale came farmers, then artisans and artists, then traders. Among all who rendered homage to the great lords, the warriors and their chiefs were the elite and the rest were commoners. Lines of cleavage were clearly drawn.

The *samurai* of Japanese tradition have been compared to the romanticized knights of medieval Europe and their exploits lauded through the centuries. They had an ethical code, based partly on Confucianism and Buddhism, which emphasized loyalty as the cardinal virtue. The warrior was required to sacrifice his life, and even his family, if the service of his lord required it. It was a code which could be, and often was harsh, humorless and even positively cruel. One of its chief characteristics, points out a leading authority, was indifference to the rights of the individual. It "taught a vassal to sacrifice his own interest and his own life on the altar of loyalty, but it did not teach a ruler to recognize the rights of the ruled. It taught a wife to efface herself for her husband's sake, but it did not teach a husband any corresponding obligation towards a wife. In a word, it expounded the relation of the whole to its parts, but left unexpounded the relations of the parts to one another." [2]

Although it has been idealized in modern times as *Bushido*, the chivalry of the feudal period in Japan was largely a code of simple militarism. "To be sure," frankly states the Japanese scholar Uichi Iwasaki, "much sentimentality developed about it, and crude brutality was largely eliminated; but at the bottom was the sword and nothing else. *Bushido* taught that the sword of the *samurai* was his honor, which was dearer to him than his life. The sword was a symbol of God. For ten centuries the nation was engulfed in this tradition. What wonder that the Japanese today are inclined to be militaristic? It has been said that the militarism of Japan was imported from Germany. Japan was a military nation before she ever heard of Germany. What happened was this: the devotees of the old military spirit, seeking a means of expression in the modern world, saw the Prussian scheme of militarization, found it good, and adapted it as far as possible to Japan." [3]

Generally speaking, the *samurai* appears to have been

a rough, illiterate sort of fellow whose habits and outlook bore little relation to the glorified concept presented by Dr. Inazo Nitobe, author of *Bushido, The Soul of Japan*, first published in about 1905 and repeatedly reprinted for the benefit of Western readers. Dr. Nitobe outlined ethical virtues, allegedly based upon Confucian teachings, which are said to have prevailed among the *samurai* of the feudal period and which now constitute the moral instincts of the Japanese race. It may be doubted, however, whether the average *samurai* knew much about Confucius until he was forced by circumstances to take to book learning at the beginning of the seventeenth century. Courageous and loyal he may well have been, but if so it is probable that he practiced courage because his job demanded it rather than for its own sake as a virtue, and that he was loyal because it paid him to be so. There is little evidence that the feudal warrior had any sense of loyalty or patriotism as a natural virtue, especially towards the emperors, who were often shabbily treated by their subjects. *Bushido* is simply a loose term for a complex of customs and moral ideas which are supposed to be the standard of the warrior's conduct. It is a modern device by which the Japanese have sold to themselves and the world the belief that the code of the Japanese warrior is something uniquely high and noble.

A NEW RELIGION

"So modern a thing is it," wrote Professor Basil Hall Chamberlain, Emeritus Professor of Japanese and Philology at the Imperial University of Tokyo, in 1912, "that neither Kaempfer, Siebold, Satow, nor Rein—all men knowing their Japan by heart—ever once allude to it in their voluminous writings. The cause of their silence is not far to seek: *Bushido* was unknown until a decade or two ago! *The very word appears in no dictionary, native or foreign, before the year 1900.* Chivalrous individuals of course existed in Japan, as in all countries at every period; but *Bushido*, as an institution or a code of rules, has never existed. The accounts given of it have been fabricated out of the whole cloth, chiefly for foreign consumption. The analysis of medieval Japan's history shows that the great feudal houses, so far from displaying an excessive idealism in the matter of fealty to one emperor, one lord, or one party, did evolve the eminently practical plan of letting their different members take different sides, so that the family as a whole might come out as winner in any event and thus avoid the confiscation of its lands. Cases, no doubt, occurred of devotion to losing causes—for example, to Mikados in disgrace; but they were less common than in the more romantic West.

"Thus within the space of a short lifetime, the new Japanese religion of loyalty and patriotism has emerged into the light of day. The feats accomplished during the late war with Russia show that the simple ideal which it offers is capable of inspiring great deeds. From a certain point of view the nation may be congratulated on its new possession."[4]

Thus *Bushido* is, on the one hand, a very vague and loose tradition, and, on the other, an idealized concept of recent times. In its modern form it was introduced by the Meiji government to fill the need for a new national loyalty to bolster up the restored monarchical fabric, and it has become a very effective agency both for propagating loyalty to the throne and spreading the idea of Japan as "a nation of *samurai*."

Carefully inculcated into the new conscript armies organized at the end of the nineteenth century and recruited largely from the lower classes, the *Bushido* myth first began to attract attention abroad at the time of the Russo-Japanese war in 1905 when an explanation was sought for Russia's defeat at the hands of pygmy Japan. Alfred Stead, a well-known British war correspondent, wrote extravagantly in 1906: "We recognize almost grudgingly and in spite of ourselves the existence of a moral force that appears to be able to govern and sway the whole conduct of a whole people, inspiring not a caste, but a nation, from highest to lowest, to deeds that are worthy to rank with the most famous of history or legend. We want to know what this force is, whence it comes, and what it means; the sense of its existence makes us jealous, uncomfortable, almost annoyed." [5]

Stead does not appear to have realized that *Bushido* contained within itself the seeds of danger for the West, for, deprecating the existence of any such possibility, he wrote in another passage: "Is it not reasonable to suggest that the nations of the world may look with more equanimity upon the future of Japan, knowing that since the Japanese have been reared in an atmosphere charged with the moral ideas of *Bushido*, unnecessary wars will, wherever possible, be mitigated? Is such a nation likely to abuse the power she possesses and is acquiring as another nation without the same privileges might be?"[6]

Within a decade Japan had provided the answer by annexing Korea and by attempting, in 1915, to bring China under her sway at a time when the Western powers were at each other's throats in Europe. It is clear that, by creating unity and slavish obedience, *Bushido* has rather served as a spur to aggressive tendencies. This is hardly surprising in view of the fact that present-day *Bushido* is built around the idea that the Japanese race, because of its *samurai* qualities, has a divine mission to perform in the East and throughout the whole world.

THE MIKADO MYTH

Out of feudalism developed a political organization which was calculated to safeguard the interests and powers of the ruling classes.

At seeming variance with this was the unlimited sovereignty accorded to a single Emperor. From early mythology sprang the legend that he was descended directly from the Sun Goddess, and, indeed, that the nation as a whole was, in some lesser degree, of divine origin. By this legend the ruling line was clothed with a divine dignity which made disloyalty a sacrilege.

To a stanch Japanese the present Emperor is not simply Hirohito, but O-Tenshi-Sama, Son of Heaven. In the view of the hundred per cent Japanese patriot he should rule the world—and would, but for the perversity of mankind. Any denial of his divine descent, any challenge of the theory by which he reigns supreme, would court the charge of treason.

Actually, during the early history of the Japanese state, belief in the celestial origin of the Emperor was skillfully exploited by ministers who, controlling the throne, wished to bolster its loose authority. Centuries later, by an astute move, the same belief was made a basis for removing the Emperor from the sordid responsibilities of active administration and establishing a dual authority wherein real power was vested in a regent who in theory acted only *for* the Emperor. Throughout the greater part of a millennium this strange duality in government persisted. Although the regency might change hands, as it did, the sacrosanct prestige of the Emperor was maintained.

To the regent, or *shogun*, the support of the imperial prerogative thus assured was of immense advantage. It lent to his actions something of the inviolability and infallibility of the Emperor himself. All of the intense devotion and loyalty of the people to their divine sovereign served to buttress the position of those who were empowered to act for him. Thus the economic and social structure as a whole was invested with religious sanction.

In 1868 the Emperor was "restored" to power. Yet even since then, he has remained more of a symbol than an active force in politics. Although by the Constitution of 1890 vast imperial powers are concentrated in him who is held to spring from "a lineal succession unbroken for ages eternal," in practice these powers have remained the perquisites of those who had the political strength to use them. And powerful perquisites they remain to this day.

According to Shinto, the national faith of Japan, the Emperor is an incarnate Deity occupying much the same position as Jehovah occupies in Judaism. Shinto "has directed the beliefs of the people in such wise," points out a well-known authority, "as to undergird the Imperial throne with strong foundations of religious faith in the holy inviolability of the divinely descended ruler, thereby serving, as as effective check on radicalism and revolutionary sentiment."[7] Shinto hymns like the following one have helped to create a unified national purpose and a sense of divine mission:

"When Japan shall be empowered with the Holy Faith,
She will pacify other people as seems good to her.

Hereafter Japan shall command foreign powers,
Mark it well, all of you!

Hitherto they have been called Japan and foreign lands;
Hereafter there shall be naught but Japan."

As Hitler has done so effectively in the case of the Germans, Japan's military leaders have capitalized upon the Japanese strain of ill-defined mysticism, which thrives on blind obedience to blind doctrines. By skillful manipulation, the mental texture of the Japanese people and their religious faith and national consciousness have been so closely interwoven as to be almost incapable of separation. The Japanese authorities have succeeded in surrounding a doctrine of political absolutism with the final sanction of a religious belief.

MASS REGIMENTATION

Japanese patriotism, seen in the willingness of the nation's soldiers to sacrifice themselves on the battlefield and in the unity of national thought when pressure is exerted from abroad, is an aspect of Shinto which goes back to feudal times when there was an extraordinary regimentation of the individual. It was a regimentation not only of his economic and political activities, but of his intellectual and spiritual life as well. This was particularly true among the *samurai*, who were, except in times of fighting, the leisured class. The institutional complex which so rigidly commanded and subordinated the individual was adjusted primarily to a maintenance of the power of the great lords and to the dictates of group action for survival and supremacy in a militaristic feudal order. Obedience, more willing no doubt on the part of the *samurai* than of the working populace (who sometimes rebelled when food became scarce) was deeply instilled. The people as a whole were rendered mentally and ethically passive.

The capacity for loyalty and obedience remained deep-rooted in the Japanese character through all the vicissitudes of national political evolution. When, toward the end of the twelfth century, an administrative prodigy, Yorimoto, established himself as regent with the title "barbarian-subduing-general" (*shogun* for short), he organized the national power won through a closely-knit system of military constables and tax collectors. The Emperor's exalted position was maintained, and the people became increasingly conscious of a potent and sacred object for allegiance above and beyond the great lords. For immediate, practical purposes, however, the *daimyo* was still supreme.

In the sixteenth century Toyotomi Hideyoshi, sometimes called the "Japanese Napoleon," consolidated the military power of the Empire and dreamed of expansion abroad, actually carrying through an expedition to Korea. He was followed, after a period of dissension, by Iyeyasu and an able line of succeeding administrators who inaugurated, under the Tokugawa shogunate, an elaborate system of governmental supervision over the life of the people. All classes of society were subjected to minute and exact regulations, and the habit of obedience to centralized as well as local authority was firmly established.

Nobody can hope to comprehend present-day Japan unless he first studies the history of the long period of seclusion under the Tokugawa *shoguns* which preceded the imperial restoration in 1868. The two and a half centuries of Tokugawa rule saw the establishment of certain well-defined patterns of conduct that continue to shape the life and thought of the nation in modern times. Among them was the code under which each individual rendered slavish obedience to his superior so that he might in turn establish his claim to authority over those below him. In China moral excellence was the accepted criterion of fitness to rule; in Japan morality had little to do with the case. The code emphasized that a feudal lord should render unquestioning obedience to the will and desires of the *shogun*, whether the latter were right or wrong, just or unjust, and he exacted the same compliance from his own subordinates. The persistence of this blind reverence for authority helps to explain both the unity of Japan and the failure of the Japanese people to make any substantial progress towards democracy.

Possibly it was this regimentation, which made it extremely difficult for the individual to break through, that restricted Japanese development in the broader human spheres. While Japan has made some notable contributions along artistic and scientific lines, she has not given to the world a single political, religious or moral idea that has been of benefit to the human race at large.

The feudal-military order which was Japan's social and political system for a full millennium—almost all of her known history—endured beyond the brink of Japan's modern era, and the character, habits, and attitudes developed within that order have continued as potent forces ever since. Amid all the outward utilitarian changes of commercialism, industrialism, and political and social reorganization, the influences of a highly developed feudal mentality have remained strong. Thus there exists in Japan totalitarianism of a peculiarly traditional and religious quality. For the Japanese people, devotion to the military state has tended to be the primary loyalty, to a degree seldom reached even in the nationalistic West.

II

Borrowings from Abroad

THE Japanese were originally hunters and fishers and they took to agriculture only at a fairly late stage of their development. That was perhaps the reason why they were so long in developing a civilization, and then borrowed largely from abroad—chiefly from China.

China represents, on the other hand, one of the world's greatest primary civilizations. During the Shang dynasty (traditionally 1766-1122 B.C.)—nearly 2,000 years before Christ and at about the time of Abraham and Helen of Troy—the Chinese had a highly developed culture which expressed itself, among other ways, in the most exquisite bronze, ivory and gold work. The earliest surviving Chinese written records date back to about 1300 B.C., and China's oldest classical literature to about 1000 B.C.

Although fairly old according to Western standards, Japan has an authentic history (as distinguished from myth and legend) only about half as long as that of China. A Chinese record of the first century of our era is the first positive knowledge we have of the Japanese, whose chronology becomes tolerably exact only after the end of the fifth century A.D., while her earliest literary work (the *Kojiki* or *Record of Ancient Matters*) dates only from the year 712 A.D.

Although February 11 in the year 660 B.C. is officially recognized in Japan as the day on which the Japanese Empire was founded, modern historians, including the late Professor Yoshi S. Kuno, believe that the actual date was about the beginning of the Christian era. Professor Kuno declares that prior to the fifth century A.D., when Japan came into contact with Korea (then a part of the old Chinese Empire), "she was a military nation without any elements of civilization. During the fifth and sixth centuries the country came under the intellectual influence of Korea and of Korean *émigrés* to Japan. In those centuries, if Japan had anything worthy of the name of civilization, it was to be attributed to Korean efforts. In the seventh century Japan came into contact with China and entered the Period of Imitation of China and Things Chinese. She made noteworthy progress both intellectually and industrially. But the Japanese civilization of that time was merely a transplantation of the Chinese civilization." [1]

Thus in the days of Confucius the islanders were still unlettered tribesmen. When Japan grew into civilization, it was under the tuition of China, even by wholesale adoption of Chinese culture. Writing itself and the elaboration of language; models in philosophy, history, poetry, painting, sculpture, architecture, color-printing, music; legal systems, administrative patterns, court ceremonies and costumes; Confucian concepts of the family and loyalty to superiors, the ethics of self-culture, Buddhist movements even to details of sects; crafts and manual skills, medical and astronomical knowledge, social fundamentals like printing and coinage—all these were taken over from China, and the marks of them are still to be found in Japanese culture. The world rarely, if ever, witnessed such a speedy and amazing assimilation of an alien culture until Japan herself repeated the achievement in the nineteenth century, this time with the civilization of the West.

NOT BLIND IMITATION

Whether or not it be true that this tremendous task was accomplished at the cost of a more gradual development which might in the end have yielded a more original and truly creative civilization is a large and somewhat academic question which cannot be entered into here. It is important to note, however, that in the realm of political philosophy Japan has tended in each case to take over the *form* of the borrowed culture while rejecting, either consciously or unconsciously, the underlying spirit. That is one important reason why so many fundamental differences continue to exist, not only between the Japanese and the Chinese peoples, but also between the Japanese and the Western democracies.

Dr. Chikao Fujisawa, Professor of the Great Oriental Culture College of Tokyo, interprets this as evidence of "exquisite mental power." "In effect," he declares, "Japan has absorbed first Chinese civilization and culture, then the Buddhistic culture of India, and lastly Western civilization. Each time Japan came into exotic civilizations and cultures, her national thought became for the time being topsy-turvy, but in due course of time these exotic cultures became assimilated with her original culture. At present, we are endeavoring to purify and settle the turbidity that has been brought upon our own culture through our hasty importation of Western civilizations since the Meiji era. . . ."

"This is an exquisite mental power with which the Japanese embody new knowledge and culture without losing their original individuality. In fact, Japan has absorbed the world civilizations without running the risk of being absorbed by them. . . . It has been our established tradition to study alien culture without impairing our *Yamato* spirit. . . ."[2]

The Japanese were not blind imitators, it seems, but often modified the borrowed institutions in order to adapt them to the political, social and economic conditions prevailing in Japan. These changes proved so fundamental that within a century or two the similarity between Chinese and Japanese forms of government became mostly superficial. It meant that instead of following the strong scholarly, humanistic and democratic tradition established in China the Japanese continued to be largely feudalistic in outlook, with power concentrated in the hands of a governing class and with a disproportionate emphasis upon the glorification of martial valor.

ARISTOCRACY PRESERVED

Since the year 221 B.C., when the state of Ch'in succeeded in conquering the last of the remaining feudal kingdoms and for the first time in history created a unified Chinese empire, there has been virtually no feudalism in China, the military playing a subordinate and even at times an insignificant role. Several devices were employed for keeping feudalism in check. The landed aristocracy was weakened, for example, by abolishing the law of primogeniture and dividing the hereditary fief equally among the sons of a deceased or banished prince. This tended to bring about a social structure in which there were practically no class divisions, nor any enduring differences between rich and poor.[3] The restrictions on noble privilege were powerfully reinforced by the unique Chinese examination system by which, as early as the second century B.C., men were selected for public office through a competitive examination designed to test their knowledge of the classical literature of ancient China. Although criticized on some grounds, chiefly that it stressed the development of memory at the expense of original thought, the system did give China a certain democracy such as hardly existed elsewhere until recent times. It was not, of course, democracy as we understand the word today, yet it did mean democracy of a sort, since it took the government of the country away from the aristocratic and wealthy classes and placed it in the hands of anyone, high or low, who could pass the examinations.

But in Japan the leveling influence of this system was defeated by the rigid barriers by which the Japanese aristocracy surrounded itself. The Japanese observed the letter of the law, but destroyed its spirit by permitting only individuals of a certain social status to take the examinations. As a consequence, Japanese society evolved into a closely knit feudalistic system in which all the power lay in the hands of a small, comparatively unchanging class which has maintained much of its force right up to the present day. The fact that the army is still dominated by the former adherents of the fief of Choshu, and the navy by the Satsuma clan, shows the tenacious influence of the feudal military caste.

The governing classes developed, as the late Dr. Karl Robert Reischauer has pointed out, "an excellent technique of making use of every last drop of loyalty it could wring from the common people, but too often betrayed this devotion. Shinto emphasis on ancestry tended to concentrate political, economic and social privileges in the hands of a closed aristocracy that grew progressively more self-satisfied, more grasping and more incompetent until it destroyed itself time and again by its own weakness and corruption. The confidence of Confucianism in the natural goodness of man with the corresponding lack of that deep sense of sin or of failure to live up to one's highest ideals, and the Confucian emphasis on the aristocracy of virtue, tended to make the governing class smugly complacent, loudly stressing the duties of inferiors to be filial and loyal while speaking *pianissimo* about the concomitant responsibilities of superiors to be benevolent and just. . . . When unscrupulous men were in power there was no way that the common man had of protecting himself from their tyranny, for officials were frequently, in practice, above the law. Instead of being considered the fathers of their people, such officials were more often likened to beasts of prey."[4]

"RIGHT OF REVOLUTION" REJECTED

Another theory of government evolved by the Chinese but rejected in Japan was the Confucian doctrine of the Right of Revolution, clearly defined by Mencius, the great follower of Confucius, in the third century B.C. According to this doctrine the Chinese ruler was theoretically the wielder of absolute power, but it was a power circumscribed by important limitations. Although the ruler was given the exalted title of "Son of Heaven," this did not mean that he was himself regarded as a divine being; he was, rather, merely the man upon whom Heaven had for the time being conferred its Mandate or Decree to rule the empire. So long as he ruled successfully, he was regarded as enjoying heavenly support, but if he began to rule very badly, this was viewed as a positive indication that he had lost the Mandate of Heaven. Thereupon it was up to anyone who could do so to overthrow him and to establish another royal line which could once again enjoy the support of Heaven. The recognition of this doctrine is evidenced by the humble and even apologetic tone in the imperial proclamations issued by many Chinese rulers, and the boldness of the criticisms made by their Confucian advisers. It helps also to explain the numerous dynastic changes that have taken place in China and the consequent rise to prominence of many families of humble origin.

Naturally, this sort of doctrine did not meet with favor in Japan, where the Shinto emphasis upon blood proved stronger than the democratic Confucian emphasis upon virtue. It was attacked with particular vehemence by the Shinto revivalists in the eighteenth century. "The 'Holy Men' of China," wrote Norinaga Motoori (1730-1801), "were merely successful rebels. The Mikado is the sovereign appointed by the pair of deities, Izanagi and Izanami, who created this country. The Sun-goddess never said, 'Disobey the Mikado if he be bad,' and therefore, whether he be good or bad, no one attempts to deprive him of his authority. He is the immovable ruler who must endure to the end of time, as long as the sun and moon continue to shine. In ancient language the Mikado was called a god, and that is his real character. Duty therefore consists in obeying him implicitly without questioning his acts. During the middle ages, such men as Hou-den Yoshitoki, Hou-den Yasutoki, Ashikaga Taka-uji and others violated this duty (*michi*), and took up arms against him. Their disobedience to the Mikado is attributable to the influence of Chinese learning." [5]

Modern Japanese commentators are equally critical. "Loss of kingly rank does not depend merely upon the character of the ruler," says Mr. Yutaka Hibino in his *Nippon Shindo Ron*, or *The National Ideals of the Japanese People*, published as recently as 1928. "If the contention of Mencius is correct, then to banish a king, who has forfeited his authority through inefficiency or a vain display of power, is similar to banishing an ordinary subject. . . . Here ruler has always been ruler and subject subject. No subject has ever aspired to be a ruler. Why is it that no subject of this Empire has ever manifested this type of aspiration? This phenomenon is no mysterious or inexplicable thing. We must recognize here one of the special virtues and peculiar beauties which adorn our sacred Empire. Our people have ever regarded the Emperor as Emperor, and from generation to generation they have served him, desiring nothing better than to die for his sake. They have never ventured even in dreams to regard their Emperor as a common or vulgar mortal. This ancient lord and vassal relation, so full of virtue, has never fallen into desuetude, and still remains the unique glory of the Japanese nation." [6]

MILITARISM EMPHASIZED

After China had become a united nation under Ch'in Shih-huang in the third century B.C., the soldier began gradually to lose caste, and emphasis was transferred to literary and moral attainments. Political, religious, and social factors combined to suppress manifestations of the martial spirit. Both the Confucian and the Taoist schools emphasized the importance of habits of peace and order, and disapproved cultivation of the arts of war. The popular attitude towards militarism came to be epitomized in a popular proverb: "No good iron will be made into a nail; no good son will make a soldier." Here and there, as in the case of some of the T'ang poets and such popular romances as *The Three Kingdoms*, one finds a certain enthusiasm for the adventure and panoply of war, but, viewed as a whole, Chinese thought and philosophy reveal a strongly antimilitarist tinge. It took the Japanese invasion of 1937 to raise the prestige of the military man in China.

In Japan, on the other hand, the extreme development of feudalism, which was accompanied by a great deal of warfare, caused much stress to be laid upon the arts of war and upon the so-called manly and military virtues. "From the ninth to the nineteenth century," declares Dr. Uichi Iwasaki, "Japan was ruled by the sword. The power of the state was the military power. The ruling classes were the military classes. The *shogun* ruled the lords because he could defeat them in battle. The *daimyo* ruled their territories by the power of the sword; and any *samurai* could slay at will any *heimin* (commoner). The *samurai* never traveled abroad unarmed."[7]

The education of the *samurai* came to be very thorough, beginning from early childhood and including not only the arts of war but also, in later times, a system of intellectual, moral, and religious teaching. For his benefit the Confucian ethic of loyalty, honor and obedience was translated into military terms and embellished with romantic tales such as the story of the Forty-seven *Ronin*, whose influence on modern Japanese thought it is impossible to overestimate.

WESTERN INFLUENCES

By the time that Commodore Perry came upon the scene in 1853, Chinese civilization had been largely discredited and influential groups were looking for something new. Eager to make their country powerful, so that Japan might be able to preserve her political independence, the leaders of the new imperial regime that overthrew the Tokugawa shogunate sought a reason for the Westerner's military strength and great economic wealth.

European political doctrines were examined for ideas which might be usefully employed in reforming the government. Rousseau's philosophy of the social contract, the utilitarian theories of John Stuart Mill and Adam Smith, and the American Declaration of Independence were all carefully studied but were rejected by the ruling classes as being too dangerously democratic. The oligarchy found in Germany the concept best suited to their purpose and they decided upon a constitutional monarchy, with suitable modifications to meet Japanese conditions. In 1881 the Emperor issued an Imperial Decree promising the establishment of an Imperial Diet in 1890.

Once again, however, the Japanese leaders were careful to protect the traditional Japan, and hence their hold over the people, from corrosion by the new civilization. Upon his return to Japan in August, 1883, one of the first acts of Count Hirobumi Ito, who had been sent to Europe in 1882 to study the constitutions of Western nations preparatory to drafting the Japanese document, was to create the orders of prince, marquis, count, viscount, and baron. The new nobility was made up of members of the former aristocracy and of those who had distinguished themselves by conspicuous services during or after the Restoration. Thus strong support was assured from the aristocratic and official classes.

Expedience demanded that the Constitution should appear modern but should yet perpetuate and safeguard the doctrine of national polity which identifies the Emperor with the state and the state with the Emperor. It was quite obviously, says Reischauer, "a gift of the Emperor to his people; not something they had deserved or won, but something that had been granted to them through his bounteous mercy. Not even a pretense was made that this was to be a government of, for, or by the people. The Constitution was promulgated in a spirit of autocracy and has been interpreted in such a spirit with but slight and temporary changes ever since."[8]

Modeled upon the Constitution of Prussia, with which Ito had been greatly impressed, the document was provided with additional safeguards to prevent control of the Emperor and his advisers by the people's representatives. The Cabinet was made responsible not to the Diet but to the Emperor, which meant that the power remained in the hands of the oligarchy. Every loophole which might have permitted the growth of democratic rights and liberties was carefully closed up.

CHRISTIANITY READAPTED

Christianity also suffered a sea change when it was introduced after the reopening of Japan to foreign intercourse in the middle of the nineteenth century. In order to overcome the strong prejudice against a foreign religion, Christian workers were driven to assimilate their faith as closely as possible to accepted traditions and attitudes. A glimpse of the ingenious working out of this process is provided by the statement of Dr. Ebina, one of the most reputed Christian leaders at the beginning of the present century:

"Though the encouragement of ancestor worship cannot be regarded as part of the essential teaching of Christianity, it (Christianity) is not opposed to the notion that, when the Japanese Empire was founded, its early rulers were in communication with the Great Spirit that rules the universe. Christians, according to this theory, without doing violence to their creed, may acknowledge that the Japanese nation has a divine origin. It is only when we realize that the Imperial Ancestors were in close communication with God (the gods) that we understand how sacred is the country in which we live."[9]

The point was insisted upon that if Christ was to be introduced to the Japanese people He must be a japonified Christ. "Fully thankful to the Protestant missionaries for their praiseworthy efforts to instill the sense of the dignity of personality into the Japanese mind," wrote Professor Chikao Fujisawa in 1935, "we yet regret being compelled to point out the lack of foresight on the part of a portion of foreign missionaries who wished to translate intact into Japan those creeds and institutions which have been grown in foreign lands, the inhabitants of which are inspired by unlimited individualism, now and then trespassing on social unity. I hope that instead of the American or English Christ, the Japanese Christ will come down to this country, becoming a dear and familiar figure upon the Japanese road. Then, I am sure, a brilliant prospect will be laid before the future of Christian belief in Japan."[10]

There is also the statement made some years ago by the Reverend Miyasaki when he was secretary of the Japan Christian Church (the union of Presbyterian and related bodies):

"I believe that Japan is ordained as the Kingdom of God. If Jesus, Who made a pilgrimage to the Jewish temple at Jerusalem on the occasion of the Passover every year, had happened to live in Japan, He would have made this yearly pilgrimage to the grand shrine of Ise as His heavenly Father's abode."

Again, in 1937, a pastor in one of the leading Christian denominations said that the doctrine of the Trinity was not suitable for Japan, where Four Persons should be recognized, with the Emperor first in honor. Ironically enough, members of the patriotic societies, more noted for zeal in action than in reflection, attacked this remarkable effort in syncretism as an insult to the Emperor!

A more recent example of this practice of assimilating the Christian tradition to the local scene was the discovery in North Japan of "the grave of Christ," an event which was widely advertised in newsreel form. According to one version of this modern legend, Jesus dwelt in Japan under Shinto instruction during the period between the boyhood visit to the Temple and the beginning of the public ministry. Moreover, Jesus was not actually crucified and buried at Jerusalem, it was claimed, but a disciple or younger brother was substituted for him. Another instance was the "discovery" not long ago of the tablets of the Ten Commandments, covered with writing that was conveniently illegible.

A final example of conformity under pressure, or of accommodation to forcible nationalism in order to avoid potential conflict, may be given from the answers made in the name of the faculty of a Christian college to the recent "Osaka Questionnaire," a series of test propositions put before various Christians and Christian organizations upon the initiative of the gendarmerie in Osaka and other cities. Question No. 5 asked: "What is the relation of Imperial Rescripts and the Bible?" The answer given was: "The Rescript is an Imperial Decree. Thus it has concrete absoluteness. The Bible is believed to be the revelation of the word of the Christian God, and it reveals an absolute spirit, but sometimes lacks concrete commands for special particular cases. Hence the Christian as a subject, by cultivating through the Bible a pure faith void of self and a noble personality, prepares himself in advance so that when an Imperial Decree comes he can at any time act as it instructs."

Although Christianity is formally recognized as a religion under Article XXVIII of the Constitution, in practice a Japanese is required to be a good Shintoist first and is a Christian only second. The classic line of Shinto thought, with its insistence upon the divinity of the Emperor, is sedulously propagated by the authorities and no departure from it is tolerated. Thus religious freedom can be said to exist only in name and intellectual integrity is negated. Once again, as in the case of Chinese political philosophy and Western democratic institutions, the forces of reaction have striven to emasculate the imported culture so as to render it incapable of generating those "dangerous thoughts" of which the Japanese bureaucracy lives in mortal fear.

III

Early Expansion

THE Japanese urge towards expansion overseas, maritime as well as continental, began to find expression much earlier than is commonly supposed by that vast majority of people for whom the history of Japan begins with the Meiji Restoration in 1868. Japanese imperialism is usually thought of as a comparatively modern development which followed the opening of Japan to foreign intercourse as a result of Commodore Perry's expedition in the middle of the nineteenth century. It is suggested that in imitating the industrialization of the Occidental nations who thus rudely forced their attentions upon her, Japan found it necessary to imitate also the methods by which those nations had secured for themselves markets and sources of raw material abroad. The fact is, however, that long before Perry's arrival Japanese expansion had been, in one form or another, an important factor in the history of the Far East.

Perhaps the earlier attempts at expansion can scarcely be dubbed imperialism in the modern sense of the term. Most maritime countries have evinced that roving, acquisitive spirit which is so common among island communities. But the existence of this impulse came almost inevitably to form an element in latter-day Japanese imperialism, and it is essential to the understanding of that imperialism that its connection with past history should be realized.

PIRATICAL FORAYS

There is abundant evidence to show that Japanese pirates, known to the Chinese as *wok'ou* (literally "dwarf sea robbers"), roved the China Sea from about 1260 A.D. until they began to be displaced by a more formal type of merchant adventurer in the sixteenth century. Japanese historians have compared the activities of these seafarers to the exploits of the Portuguese, Dutch, and English buccaneers who helped enrich their respective countries towards the end of the Middle Ages. Certainly they appear to have had a common objective in their quest for treasure. The Japanese adventurers were influenced largely by the desire to obtain Chinese minted coinage, for which there was a keen demand in Japan owing to the currency shortage caused by the rapacious taxation of the feudal lords. The gold coins formerly in use in Japan had become extinct and silver coins were extremely scarce, leaving only the copper currency for common use, and this gave out when, in the reign of the Emperor Shomu, orders were issued that in every province of Japan a temple was to be built enshrining a great copper image of Buddha. The Japanese were then obliged to make up for the deficiency by selling to China such goods as oil, sulphur, swords, halberds, lacquer, etc., in return for coin, and it was for this reason that during the Ashikaga period in Japan commerce with the Ming empire was greatly encouraged.[1]

It is not clear when the Japanese pirate fleets first made their appearance but they seem to have played an important part in repelling Kublai Khan's attempts to annex Japan, first in 1274 and again seven years later when a still more elaborate expedition was dispatched. It is possible, indeed, that the Mongol invasion may have been launched partly in retaliation for Japanese piratical activities in Kublai Khan's Chinese dominions. In a sense the repulse of the Mongol expedition may be considered to mark the beginning of Japanese naval power, for the Japanese, profiting by the lessons learned through this devastating experience, began to build bigger and better ships in order to put themselves on even terms with their rivals. Thus equipped, the Japanese buccaneers, who at first had confined their attentions pretty much to Korea, now began to operate from the Liaotung peninsula to Shantung province and then on down the coast to Canton and beyond that again to the South Seas.

Many of the *wok'ou* started out as legitimate merchants and turned to piracy later under circumstances which are described as follows by a contemporary Chinese scholar quoted by the Japanese historian, Yosoburo Takekoshi: "The Japanese pirates were on the islands of the sea, and their nature was cunning and greedy. At first, during the Kobu era, they paid tribute but were not obedient. The Imperial Court first made inquiry and then discontinued intercourse as a fixed policy. In the early part of Eiraku they again came to bring tribute, armed, but carrying local products. If they got a chance they made use of their arms, but they were crafty enough to say they had come to present the local products. In case of raid they looted the treasures of the people, and in case of tribute they received presents from the country, so they were always on the right side. At the end of Sentoku they came and, getting no chance of a raid, wanted to present tribute. The Imperial Court ordered them to go to Peking without knowing their intention, and sent them away with treasures and presents on board. In Seito they again came and, seizing their chance, they entered Tocho, invaded Taiko, plundered godowns, burnt down the houses, massacred all the people, piling up dead bodies like a mountain, making blood flow like a river, pouring boiling water over babies tied to a post, amusing themselves with their cries. When they captured a pregnant woman they would wager as to whether the child in the womb was male or female and then cut it out; everywhere they abandoned themselves to dissipation and orgies of obscenity. Upon this the Imperial Court ordered preparations to be made against the pirates."[2]

FOOTHOLDS IN SOUTHERN ASIA

The bitter internal strife which preceded the unification of Japan under Nobunaga and his successors towards the end of the sixteenth century provided ample outlet at home for adventurous spirits, and the Japanese pirates gradually disappeared from the China Sea. But the national desire for expansion abroad led to the discovery of a convenient foothold in Southern Asia and in process of time the *wok'ou* gave place to the so-called "Red Mark" ships privileged by the government to go abroad. During the second half of the sixteenth century Japanese adventurers began to push down towards the southeast, some of the boldest going so far afield as the Philippine Islands, where they soon came into conflict with the Spaniards. It is recorded that, much exercised over the discriminatory treatment applied to the Japanese in the Philippines, a certain Kiemon Harada did his best to persuade Toyotomi Hideyoshi, then the real ruler of Japan, to dispatch an expedition to "take the islands at a single blow, which would increase the sale of wheat-flour and other merchandise and bring money into the country."[3]

Hideyoshi saw merit in the suggestion as possibly offering opportunities for employment for his restive followers and in 1592 he sent to the Spanish governor of the Philippines an arrogant letter which read in part as follows:

"For more than a hundred years, military leaders in all the provinces had fought with one another and had been continuously engaged in warfare. Our country had thereby lost its national unity, having been split into innumerable separate units. It had also lost communication and traffic facilities. My birth was accompanied by miraculous omens, which were interpreted by physiognomists to mean that I was destined to rule nations. This prediction has been fulfilled. Even in my youth, to control national affairs became my duty. Within less than ten years the unification of the nation was effected, not even an inch of land being left unconquered. Our national authority has been extended far beyond our borders. Korea, Liu Chiu, and other nations that are far away have sent their tribute-bearing envoys and paid homage to us. We are now undertaking the conquest of Tai-Min [China]. This step, however, is not actuated by our own inclinations, but is taken in pursuance of a heavenly command. As for your own country, we have not yet received either homage or tribute. Accordingly we have decided to send our military forces to your country to mete out due punishment. Our vessels are ready to sail to your shores. . . ."[4]

Subsequently a Spanish mission arrived in Japan with a noncommittal reply. This did not satisfy Hideyoshi, who compelled the envoys to swear that the Philippines would be submissive and faithful to him. There matters appear to have rested until 1616, when Captain Richard Cocks, an Englishman connected with the East India Company, suggested to the Japanese "Amerall of the Sea," or Naval Commander-in-Chief, that he should "put it into the Emperour's mynd to make a conquest of the Manillias, and drive those small crew of Spaniardes from thence, it being so neare unto Japan."[5] The suggestion was not acted upon at that time, but in 1630, according to Professor Kuno, the *shogun* Iyemitsu accepted a plan submitted by Matsukura, an eminent military leader, and instructed him to invade the Philippines. Matsukura died, however, and the project was abandoned. Subsequently, in 1637, a second expedition was planned with the assistance of the Dutch traders to Japan, who offered to furnish a fleet of war vessels. This was thwarted by a great Christian uprising in Kyushu and the Dutch traders, always eager to be of service, offered their fleet for the bombardment of the Christian stronghold.[6]

Towards the end of the sixteenth century the Japanese had established settlements at widely distributed points in southern Asia, competing for a foothold with the Chinese, Portuguese and Spaniards, by whom, especially in the case of the last-mentioned, they were regarded with deep distrust. The Spaniards had good cause to fear the Japanese, for in 1582 the Philippines had been invaded by a flotilla of twenty-six ships under a Japanese pirate chief named Taifusa, who landed at the mouth of the Kagayan River. Taifusa was beaten off after a fierce battle, but thereafter the Spaniards lived in terror of the Japanese adventurers and devoted much time and effort to building strong fortifications against them. It is an illuminating commentary on the persistence of the expansionist spirit in Japan that in 1942—three and a half centuries later—the Philippines should still be the object of Japanese aggression.

STRONG POSITION IN SIAM

In Siam the Japanese had won for themselves a much stronger position. Even before the arrival of the Dutch and Portuguese upon the scene in the early part of the sixteenth century Japanese pirates had already extended their activities to this region, where they looted vessels coming from India, China, and even from Japan itself. A hundred years later they were still levying toll along the Siamese coast, and it was while on his way to the Batani Strait that Captain John Davis, the English navigator, after whom the Davis Strait was named, was killed in a fight with Japanese pirates in 1604. At this time the British, through the East India Company, were trying to obtain a share of the trade with Siam which hitherto had been largely monopolized by the Dutch, but they were not successful, and in 1623 withdrew from the field.

By the beginning of the seventeenth century Japanese influence had taken deep root in Siam, both politically and socially. At that time there were resident in the country some 8,000 Japanese, who, split up into a number of self-governing groups, occupied a wide area which came to be known as the Japanese Settlement. Some of the Japanese group leaders became powerful figures in Siamese domestic politics and at least two married royal princesses. Japanese held high positions at the court and for a time the royal bodyguard was composed of Japanese soldiers of fortune.

There is a romantic story which tells how when King Parasong was on his deathbed in 1628 he called to his side Nagamasa Yamada, a Japanese adventurer who had been largely instrumental in putting him onto the throne, and commanded him to share with another Japanese named Kohama the responsibilities of the regency during the minority of the young Crown Prince. But Parasong's widow took Kohama, who was young and handsome, as her lover, and for his sake poisoned the boy king, who was thirteen years old, and seized the throne herself. Subsequently the Queen had Yamada poisoned also, and this led to a quarrel with the Japanese which finally resulted in the latter's withdrawal from Siam in a fleet of 300 ships in 1633.[7] Yamada's exploits were recalled in a propaganda film made in

Japan a few years ago for display in Siam as a means of promoting good will between the two countries on the basis of their traditional relationship.

There is evidence, too, of Japanese settlement in Java during the sixteenth century, and in 1619, when an English fleet attacked Jakatra, they found that Japanese troops were assisting the Dutch to defend the port. Numbers of Japanese emigrated also to Cambodia, where, in about 1637, there were some seventy or eighty Japanese families upon whom the Court appears to have relied a good deal for support in time of domestic emergency.

HIDEYOSHI'S DREAM OF EMPIRE

It seems likely that the exploits of these intrepid adventurers may have helped to inspire the expansionist ambitions of Hideyoshi, who, on his occasional visits to Sakai, the seaport near Kyoto which was the headquarters of the principal trading interests, used to hear stirring tales of adventure in China and the Philippines. These stories may well have helped to feed the ambition which led him to invade Korea in 1592, and again in 1597, in the hope of using it as a gateway for the conquest of China. His pretext for these futile and costly expeditions was the discontinuance of the practice of sending Korean embassies to Japan, but in reality, as his biographers have made clear, he was influenced largely by an innate love of foreign conquest. That Hideyoshi's objective was the subjugation of China there can be little doubt, for so far back as 1578 he was reported to have made this boastful declaration to his master, Nobunaga:

"When I have conquered the Chugoku, I will go on to Kyushu and take the whole of it. When Kyushu is ours, if you will grant me the revenue of that island for one year, I will prepare ships of war and supplies and go over and take Korea. Korea I shall ask you to bestow on me as a reward for my services, and to enable me to make still further conquests; for with Korean troops, aided by your illustrious influence, I intend to bring the whole of China under my sway. When that is effected the three countries (China, Korea and Japan) will be one. I shall do it all as easily as a man rolls up a piece of matting and carries it under his arm."[8]

Hideyoshi's plans actually extended far beyond the conquest of China. "His aim," says Professor Kuno, "was to create a great Asiatic empire, including China, Japan, Korea, India, Persia and such other Asiatic nations as were known to the Japanese in those days, as well as all the islands near the continent, such as the Liu Chiu, Formosa, the Philippines, and other islands in the South Sea. He planned first to extend his ruling authority over China, Japan and Korea, together with the surrounding islands, and to make them the first unit of his new empire."[9]

In 1590, his ambition still unfulfilled, Hideyoshi visited the shrine of Yoritomo at Tsurugoaka, near Kamakura, and, patting the image of the great *shogun* familiarly on the back, addressed it in these terms: "You are my friend! You took all the power under heaven (in Japan). You and I only have been able to do this. But you were of high and illustrious descent and not like me, sprung from peasants. But as for me, after conquering all the Empire, I intend to conquer China. What do you think of that?"[10]

Psychologists might find in this an interesting historical example of the "compensating thrust" commonly associated with a social inferiority complex. But in addition to his megalomaniacal desire to impress posterity Hideyoshi was moved by a much more practical consideration—the need to find employment for the military chieftains who, united under his control, were threatening to get out of hand. "Hideyoshi's power to give," points out Rai Sanyo in his *Nihon Gwaishi*, "was limited by the size of the country over which he ruled, and consequently it came about that rewards for his generals had to be sought in other lands. Accordingly, before the wounds received in the battles they had fought in their own country were healed, his generals were despatched to Korea—a country entirely unknown to them—where during a series of years they spent their strength in a fruitless war."[11]

At one stage of the Korean campaign there were as many as 200,000 Japanese serving overseas. Although the enterprise ended in failure after six years of desultory but exhausting warfare, it is considered by some Japanese historians to have been indirectly beneficial. It is pointed out that the national spirit was greatly stimulated and, economically, a tremendous fillip was given to the ironworking industries. The great prosperity of the Japanese trade with southern China and neighboring regions when the Tokugawa family took over the helm of state in Japan after Hideyoshi's death in 1598 is attributed to the progress of shipbuilding brought about by the invasion.[12]

IV

Imperialism under the Tokugawas

For a time, Iyeyasu, the first of the Tokugawa *shoguns*, also made national expansion the fundamental policy of his government. Whereas his predecessor, Hideyoshi, had set out to found a great empire on the Asiatic continent by military conquest, however, Iyeyasu planned to make Japan one of the great commercial centers of the world. To this end he encouraged Japanese seafarers to venture so far afield as South America and Europe, and induced traders from the outside world to come to Japan. Iyeyasu appears to have been remarkably successful in building up Japan's overseas trade, for in the early part of the seventeenth century Japanese ships plied continuously between the harbors of Japan and those of India, the Malay Peninsula, Siam, Annam, Java, Sumatra, the Philippines, Cambodia, Cochin China, Formosa, Borneo and Macao.[1]

He gradually changed his policy towards one of seclusion, however, and after his death in 1616 his successors, Hidetada and Iyemitsu, sealed up the country against any but the most carefully regulated intercourse with foreign countries. Had they continued Iyeyasu's policy of commercial expansion Japan might well have acquired three centuries ago, by more or less peaceful means, the *Lebensraum* which she is now seeking belatedly to acquire by force. But they deliberately abandoned the far-flung settlements that had been established abroad, prohibiting the Japanese settlers there from returning to Japan under penalty of death.

Professor Kuno has expressed the view that if the course of events had not been diverted in this way the Japanese might have established colonies along the coast of Siberia and extended their domain down the coast of Asia, beginning at Kamchatka in the north and running southward to the Philippines, Borneo, Java, and Sumatra. There was also the possibility, he feels, that Japan might have established settlements in Lower California more than a century before the United States of America became an independent nation. "Japan had been feared in Asiatic waters," he points out, "for approximately two hundred years, beginning in the early part of the fifteenth century when Japanese pirates had ravaged and controlled the coasts of China and Korea. In fact, Japan had thus exercised control over Asiatic waters a century before modern European nations had sought to establish authority in Asia. Therefore, the rise of Japan in the seventeenth and eighteenth centuries as the great power in Asiatic waters, a rise which might have been comparable to that of Great Britain in European waters, would have been an accomplished historical fact if Japan had not secluded herself in 1639."[2]

TROUBLE WITH CHRISTIANS

It was because of increasing trouble with the Catholic missionaries who accompanied the foreign traders, Professor Kuno suggests, that the Tokugawa *shoguns* turned towards a policy of national seclusion as the only guaranty for the safe existence of their government and nation. But, apart from the uncomfortable possibility that some day Japan might be invaded, there was, too, the risk that if foreign commerce were allowed to continue unchecked the southern trading clans might become powerful enough to threaten the position of the shogunate. The Tokugawas, who had in mind only one objective—the stabilization of their family power—therefore decided to isolate the country from foreign contacts. Japanese ships were prohibited from going abroad and Japanese residents overseas were forbidden to return to Japan. Thus a halt was called to the expansionist activities which had been carried on intensively for more than a century, and the widely scattered Japanese settlements in the southern Pacific area disappeared.

Although it was not the only reason, the penetration of Christian influence into Japan unquestionably had much to do with this remarkable *volte-face*. By 1614 nominal Christian converts are said to have numbered about 1,000,000—some authorities put the figure as high as 2,000,000—and it was feared that the Spaniards might use them as a "fifth column." Iyemitsu therefore promulgated a series of anti-Christian laws under which converts were subjected to increasingly brutal tortures until finally, in 1638, Christianity was practically blotted out. Professor Kuno admits that this inhuman persecution reflected upon the national honor and dignity of Japan, though perhaps it was no worse than the horrors inflicted by the Spanish Inquisition in the name of Christianity itself.

"Sometimes," he writes, "the backs of Christians were slashed open with dull knives, and boiling water was poured into these openings until the victims fainted. After they had been revived, the same treatment was repeated; and so on until death brought relief. Sometimes, groups of Christians, after having been subjected to agonizing torture, were driven up to the slope of a volcano, where they were thrown down the slopes of the crater and rolled slowly down to the fire below.

"Again, after both the hands and legs of the Christians had been slowly sawed off with dull bamboo saws, their bodies were rolled up and down hills until death came. Yet again, the fingers and toes of the Christians were chopped off, after which the hands and legs were tied together and exposed to snow or ice until the sufferers died of freezing. Sometimes these victims were piled into small boats, which drifted out to sea. The Christians of those days called Iyemitsu the 'Nero of Japan.' When these methods of persecution became known to the priests in Manila, they came to Japan in greater numbers, as if they wished to grasp the opportunity to die as Christian martyrs. Finally, priests began to come from Rome, Lisbon, and Madrid, their sole desire being to engage in missionary work in Japan, though it meant certain death."[3]

SHINTO REVIVAL

But the expansionist spirit did not die out during the two and a half centuries of seclusion under the Tokugawa rule. It remained dormant and was fanned into fresh activity by the revival of Shintoism which began in the seventeenth century as a reaction against Chinese philosophy and developed a religio-nationalism that has persisted until modern times. It was in the course of this revival that "the dogma of the divine origin, not merely of the Imperial line, but of the entire Japanese people, and even of the seas and soil of Japan, was, if not first formulated, at all events militantly and uncompromisingly insisted upon. All outside peoples were evil-hearted, unclean barbarians; and the very presence of such in the sacred land of the gods was contamination. . . ."[4] The leader of the movement, which reached its climax towards the end of the eighteenth century, was Norinaga Motoori, whose arrogant attitude towards the Chinese was summed up in the following dictum:

"The Japanese are instinctively and naturally noble and virtuous—not like the Chinese, who require a clumsy and artificial system of ethical philosophy for the cultivation of their moral natures."[5]

In a work entitled *The Spirit of Straightening*, written in 1771, Motoori developed the idea that, since the Mikado is the divine descendant of the gods, Japan ranks far above all other countries and therefore all are bound to do homage to the Japanese sovereign. His thesis has been summarized by Sir Ernest Satow as follows:

"Japan is the country which gave birth to the Goddess of the Sun, Amaterasu-Oho-mi-kami, which fact proves its superiority over all other countries which also enjoy her favors. The goddess, having endowed her grandson, Ninigi No Mikoto, with the three sacred treasures, proclaimed him sovereign of Japan for ever and ever. His descendants shall continue to rule it as long as the heavens and earth endure. Being invested with this complete authority, all the gods under heaven and all mankind submitted to him, with the exception of a few wretches who were quickly subdued.

"To the end of time, each Mikado is the goddess' son. His mind is in perfect harmony of thought and feeling with hers. He does not seek out new inventions but rules in accordance with precedents which date from the age of the gods, and if he is ever in doubt, he has recourse to divination, which reveals to him the mind of the great goddess. In this way the age of the gods and the present age are not two ages, but one, for not only the Mikado but also his ministers and people act up to the tradition of the divine age. . . ."[6]

Similar sentiments are to be found in the writings of Motoori's most famous pupils, Nakatsune Hatori and Atsutane Hirata. "Our country," wrote the former in 1791, "owing to the facts that it was begotten by the two gods Izanagi and Izanami, was the birthplace of Amaterasu Oho-mi-kami, and is ruled by her Sublime Descendants for ever and ever, as long as the universe shall endure, is infinitely superior to other countries, whose chief and head it is: its people are honest and upright of heart and are not given to useless theorizing and falsehood like other countries, and thus it possesses correct and true information with regard to the origin of the universe. This information has descended to us unaltered from the age of the gods, and unmixed, even in the slightest degree, with unsupported notions of individuals. This indeed is the genuine and true tradition . . ."[7]

Hirata, who lived from 1776 to 1843, carried on the tradition. The rest of the world, he contended, was made up of the inferior material left over after Izanagi and Izanami had finished the job of creating divine Japan. "As it was Japan which lay directly opposite to the sun when it had sprouted upwards and separated from the earth," he declared, "it is quite clear that Japan lies on the summit of the globe. It is equally evident that all other countries were formed at a much later period by the spontaneous consolidation of the foam of the sea and the collection of mud in various localities when Izanagi and Izanami brought forth the eight islands of Japan, and separated the land from the water. Foreign countries were of course produced by the power of the creator gods, but they were not begotten by the sun, which is the cause of their inferiority. . . . The fact is patent that the Mikado is the true Son of Heaven, who is entitled to reign over the four seas and the ten thousand countries."[8]

SHOIN YOSHIDA

From this Shinto revival there sprang an imperialist movement which sought to remind the nation of the aims of Greater Japan. The writings of Motoori and his school profoundly influenced the leaders of the expansionist movement which marked the end of the Tokugawa regime. Among the most effective of these protagonists was a remarkable individual who has been made known to English readers by Robert Louis Stevenson[9] as Yoshida Torajiro, though he is known more commonly as Shoin Yoshida or Yoshida Shoin.

Yoshida was unquestionably one of the most outstanding figures of the movement which in 1868 overthrew the shogunate and restored the Imperial authority. "If we are going to speak of the Restoration," Mr. Iichiro Tokutomi[10] points out in his biographical study, "we must necessarily speak of Yoshida Shoin. Just as a mother may die in giving birth to her child, but the child lives and grows to manhood, so we may say he was the mother and child of the Restoration."

Shoin Yoshida and his associates, who were already active by the time of Perry's arrival in 1853, advocated for Japan a program of foreign conquest including the seizure of Formosa, Korea, Manchuria, Saghalien, Kamchatka and eastern Siberia. A brilliant pupil of Shozan Sakuma, one of the earliest advocates of the opening of Japan to foreign intercourse, Yoshida was himself a teacher. Although fanatically antiforeign, he belonged to the group which, recognizing the impossibility of ignoring Western culture, sought to master Western science and apply it in Japan so as to be able to meet the foreign intruders with their own weapons. "Just now," Yoshida is quoted as having declared, "all foreigners are inquiring into our weak points. It is my greatest wish at this time that we may unite the hearts of the people of our sixty states into one body as strong as stone, and chastise the small and ugly-minded foreigners, and quiet all our troubles."[11]

Like the great Hideyoshi, who was considered to resemble a monkey, Yoshida had a singularly unprepossessing appearance. "He was ugly," Stevenson records, "and laughably disfigured with the smallpox; and while nature had been so niggardly with him from the first, his personal habits were still more sluttish. His clothes were wretched; when he ate or washed he wiped his hands upon his sleeves, and as his hair was not tied more than once in two months, it was often disgusting to behold." But he was blessed with that single-mindedness so characteristic of the race from which he had sprung. Such was his passion for study, that he "even begrudged himself natural repose; and when he grew drowsy over his books he would, if it was summer, put mosquitoes up his sleeve; and, if it was winter, take off his shoes and run barefoot in the snow."

THIRST FOR WESTERN LEARNING

For two and a half centuries until the arrival of Commodore Perry's American ships at Yedo in 1853, the Tokugawas had succeeded in maintaining a state of comparative isolation from the outside world. With an amazing tenacity of purpose Yoshida Shoin made repeated attempts to smuggle himself out of the country aboard a foreign vessel in order to study Western civilization on the spot and to extract its essence for the benefit of his country. Finally, in company with a friend, Yoshida sought to board Commodore Perry's own ship, the steam frigate *Powhatan*, which had now returned to Simoda.

Stevenson tells how in a little temple, hard by the seashore, the two conspirators lay down to repose and then, with the dawn of what was to have been their last morning in Japan, seized a fisherman's boat and rowed to the spot where Perry's ship was lying far out to sea because of the tides. "Their very manner of boarding was significant of determination; for they had no sooner caught hold upon the ship than they kicked away their boat to make return impossible. But the Commodore was already in treaty with the *Shogun's* Government; it was one of the stipulations that no Japanese was to be aided in escaping from Japan; and Yoshida and his follower were handed over as prisoners to the authorities at Shimoda. That night he who had been to explore the secrets of the barbarian slept, if he might sleep at all, in a cell too short for lying down at full length, and too low for standing upright. There are some disappointments too great for commentary."

According to the version of the episode given in the official account of Perry's expedition, the Commodore would gladly have given refuge to Yoshida and his companion if he had felt himself at liberty to indulge his own feelings. There were other considerations at stake, however. "To connive at the flight of one of the people was to disobey the laws of the Empire, and it was the only true policy to conform, in all possible regards, to the institutions of a country by which so many important concessions had already been granted."[12]

PLANS FOR EXPANSION

Six years later Shoin Yoshida was executed in connection with a conspiracy against the *shogun* and consequently he did not live to see the successful launching of the movement he had done so much to inspire. But he became a martyr in the minds of his former students and his ideas influenced many of the statesmen who guided Japan with success to unity and power during the succeeding Meiji period. Among those who came directly under Yoshida's personal influence were Count Hirobumi Ito, framer of the Japanese Constitution, and Marquis Aritomo Yamagata, founder of the modern Japanese army. In his biography of Ito, Kengi Hamada writes:

"The figure of a heroic soul, brilliant and passionate, shines forth from the dark and bloody pages of history. It is the figure of a Choshu prophet whose adherence to his lofty convictions was beyond the comprehension of his persecutors and whose invaluable life was snuffed out all to prematurely to enable him to realize his dreams. It is Sho-in Yoshida, than whom there is none greater among the tragic martyrs of Japan. . . ."

"This was the man to whom Kuruhara, Ito's *samurai* leader, himself a disciple, recommended Ito for further instruction in the classics. . . ."[13]

"Young Ito, returning west from Miyata and equipped with a mind rich with the brilliant impressions of the eastern tumult, entered the portals of the Shoka Sonjuku and began at once to receive the fiery influence of Sho-in's astounding mind. The distinguished master and the eager pupil were quick to discover in each other a community of interests, of ideals, of aspirations. Sho-in was tremendously impressed by this young recruit, and the thought raced through his mind, like water through a mill race, that here was a budding genius gifted with those very attributes of leadership which would enable him to succeed where he himself had failed in diverting the nation's course from the terrible fate to which it was obviously headed. Ito, Sho-in decided, was Japan's man of destiny. And having so decided, he proceeded to instill into this raw youth those imperishable convictions which burned in his breast."[14]

After the execution of Yoshida, young Ito placed his own silken *obi* over the decapitated body of his revered teacher in order to complete the ceremonial robes in which he was to be buried. Later, as Hamada records, he "took occasion to weigh the fundamentals, the venerable ideals of a race dedicated to something essentially higher and nobler—the spirit of *Yamato*. In this he was sustained by Sho-in's immaculate example. Sho-in had disclosed during his brief but exemplary career, this higher and nobler objective, this indispensable spiritual essence of a true patriot of *Dai Nippon*, in all its pristine brilliance."[15]

Although Yamagata studied under Yoshida Shoin only for a short while, the master's moral influence seems, according to Dr. Rikitaro Fujisawa, to have made a lasting impression upon his gifted pupil. "The first idea of the formation of the modern Japanese army," Dr. Fujisawa declares, "may be traced to Yoshida Shoin."[16]

Shoin Yoshida appears to have been strongly influenced by the writings of the *samurai* scholar, Soko

Yamaga (1622-1685), whose lectures on Confucianism and military strategy gained for him a great reputation, though his main claim to fame rests perhaps upon the fact that Oishi, the leader of the celebrated Forty-seven *Ronin*, was one of his pupils. Yamaga was a foremost exponent of the *samurai* spirit, which he set forth in a series of lectures entitled *Bukyo Shogaku*, or *Primary Military Teaching*.

"It was probably in the writings of Soko Yamaga," says Tokutomi, "that we find the chief source of Shoin's great loyalty to the Imperial House and it was the ideas of Yamaga that ran all through his discussions about his theory of the State, and the expansion of the national power and *Bushido*." [17] From this it would appear that expansionism began to be preached almost from the beginning of the Tokugawa regime, and that the spirit of Hideyoshi continued to influence generations of Japanese statesmen.

Coming at the end of a long line of scholars who had sought to establish the uniqueness of Japanese culture, Shoin Yoshida preached Japanese dominance in Asia to the exclusion of Westerners—a doctrine which has come to form one of the basic principles of Japanese policy in modern times. In his *Record of a Dark Room Prisoner*, which he penned in jail after the ignominious failure of his attempt to go abroad, Yoshida outlined a concrete program of expansion. He advocated, says Tokutomi, "the opening of the Hokkaido and establishing clan lords there, the taking of Kamchatka and the Kurile Islands and advising the Lord of Ryuku to attach them to Japan; to compel the Koreans to pay tribute to our country as in former times; to take a part of Manchuria and to take Formosa and the Loochoo Islands and gradually show an aggressive tendency."[18]

Some of Yoshida's associates favored an even broader imperialism. "Our great obligation today," declared his friend and fellow capitive, Sanai Hashimoto, "is to readjust the administration of the country and by diplomacy to develop friendly relations with some of the most important foreign countries. According to the tendency of the times, I believe there should be in future an alliance between the five great continents. The chief of this confederation will naturally be England or Russia, but I believe that it should be Russia, as England is too avaricious. Russia is strong and strict, and therefore Russia will probably make the best reputation. Japan, in order to maintain her independence, must have Korea and part of Manchuria and also should have territories in South America and India. This will be very difficult, however, as we are not strong enough yet and for this reason we should make an alliance with Russia because she is our neighbour. If we depend on Russia she will feel friendly towards us. Until this is accomplished, it would be well to seek the sympathy of America and get her help in resisting the aggression of England. In carrying out this imperial policy we must look upon America as our Eastern ally, and Russia as our brother, and Europe as our territory, and the first important thing is to take some territory in the nearest countries."[19]

WESTERN KNOWLEDGE SEEPS IN

It may be thought surprising, in view of the seclusion policy adopted by the Tokugawas, that so much should have been known of the outside world at this time. The fact is, however, that isolation from foreign contacts was far from complete. For more than two centuries, from about 1640 until about 1860, i.e. from the days of the Thirty Years' War in Europe to the period just before the outbreak of the Crimean War, Japan remained in strict, but not absolute, seclusion. Chinese books on Western science were gradually admitted.

"Among them," points out Professor Izura Shimmura, "were books on astronomy and mathematics, and although the theories contained in them were antiquated by at least a century, they were, nevertheless, welcomed by Japanese scholars. However strict the censorship was, some of the banned books found their way to the scholars in much the same way as the Christians in concealment had kept their faith through the two hundred years until the reopening of the country in the middle of the nineteenth century. It was impossible to kill either faith or scholarship. Throughout the years of strict seclusion, Western civilization kept on making whatever little contributions possible through Chinese translations of religious and scientific books, paintings, engravings, and other industrial art goods that were being imported. Thus the importation of Western science and art from China was being carried out through the thin channels of translation of writings and ideas."[20]

Apart from this indirect importation of Western knowledge, the Dutch, who alone had been allowed to continue trading at Nagasaki, under rigid restrictions, were a fruitful source of information about the outside world. They were obliged to submit to the *shogun* annual reports with regard to the condition both of Europe and the Orient, and this helped to keep the Japanese officials posted. "We may presume," Professor Shimmura declares, "that the Japanese people possessed at an earlier date a more accurate knowledge of the geography and ethnology of Europe and other continents than the Europeans did of Japan."

FRONTIERS EXTENDED

The extent to which the dreams of Shoin Yoshida have been fulfilled is a matter of common knowledge. The young leaders of the Restoration began determinedly to remodel Japan upon foreign standards, choosing only such methods in military training and education as would further the cause of nationalism in Japan and prepare for the recall of the privileges granted to foreigners in the treaties, thus placing Japan upon a footing of equality with the nations of the West. Of importance in this connection was the outbreak in 1870 of the Franco-Prussian War. Ito, who had traveled to Europe and America in search of information which might be of profit to Japan, chanced to be in Europe at the time and he found in the ideas of Hardenberg, Bismarck and Stein the models that he sought. Upon his return from abroad French instructors were replaced by German military mentors and, while it retained its *samurai* traditions, the new Japanese army was remodeled upon the Prussian system.

Japan's first attempts at continental expansion in the nineteenth century were cautiously made. Ito and his colleagues saw that the forcible acquisition of an overseas empire must be postponed until the nation's military strength had been built up, but meanwhile they lost no diplomatic opportunity that might be turned to good account. Thus, by one means or another, within a decade or two of the Restoration, the Liu Chiu Islands, the southern Kuriles and the Bonins had come into Japanese hands. But, as had been foreseen by the Tokugawas centuries earlier, expansionism is not always an unmixed blessing. The further Japan extended her control in the direction of the Asiatic mainland the closer it brought the danger of a conflict with China, and, eventually, with Tsarist Russia. Once regarded in the light of a gateway to the conquest of China, Korea now came to be fearfully envisaged as "the dagger pointed at the heart of Japan."

JAPAN'S SOUTHWARD DRIVE

Successful wars against China in 1894 and Russia ten years later greatly extended the Japanese Empire and were followed by the annexation of Korea in 1910. The outbreak of a world war in 1914 opened up fresh opportunities of expansion and Japan was quick to take advantage of them. At the Versailles Conference she put in a successful bid for the German holdings in Shantung province and for control of the Mariana, Marshall and Caroline Islands, which lay directly across the sea route from the American mainland and Hawaii to the Philippines and China, thus constituting one of the most important strategic areas in the South Seas. Twenty years later, in the course of the Sino-Japanese hostilities which grew out of her occupation of Manchuria in 1931, she was able to acquire another important foothold by occupying, in the face of ineffectual Anglo-French protests, the island of Hainan, which commands the approaches to French Indo-China.

Despite her heavy commitments in the war against China which she began in 1937, Japan lost no time in preparing to exploit the favorable situation created by the renewal of hostilities in Europe in 1939. Two months after the Second World War started a new body called the Institute of the Pacific was formed, with influential backing, to organize Japanese opinion in readiness for opportunities which the European war was confidently expected to open up. The Institute claimed a preferential position for Japan in Burma, Indo-China, and the Dutch East Indies. Its magazine pointed out that the European war provided a golden opportunity to rectify the "unjust distribution" of natural resources in the South Seas. It claimed that access to those resources was indispensable "in order to complete Japan's continental policy and to make the New Order self-sufficient."

These objectives were discussed in an article by Misao Kondo on "The European Conflict and the South Seas" in the Institute's official organ. "It is necessary," he wrote, "to rectify Japan's economic portion, and now is the psychological moment, while European powers with interests in the South Seas are preoccupied. To achieve fruition of our continental policy and make the New

Order self-sufficient it is absolutely essential to utilize the resources of the South Seas.

"From racial and geographical viewpoints Japan has the best right to the resources of these regions. Now that European influence is weakened by war, an opportunity has come to regulate the South Sea question.

"It is sometimes proposed that Dutch oil be forcibly seized, but other methods can be tried first. One method would be to demand that Japan, China and Manchukuo receive preferential access. It is unreasonable that natives should be compelled to buy expensive European goods when they want Japan's excellent and cheap goods.

". . . . Disposal of the China incident (the Chinese-Japanese War) alone cannot settle the East Asian question. To achieve East Asia's prosperity Japan must break the deadlock in her relations with the South Seas."

Subsequent events still live too vividly in the memory to require recapitulation here. Enough has been said in this brief survey to show that long before Commodore Perry's expedition opened up Japan to foreign intercourse the Japanese were already impregnated with imperialistic ideas which were partly of religious origin and tinged with mysticism. After 1853 this indigenous chauvinism was intensified by pressure from and contact with the West. The military spirit it generated was receptive to Western ideas of power and prestige, while the encroachment of European nations in China and, to a less extent, in Japan itself, indicated what might be expected if the nation was not prepared to defend its sovereign rights. As the possibilities of Asiatic dominance were conceived, the ancient sense of destiny crystallized into Pan-Asianism, reinforced by religious sanction and loyalty to the Emperor, which has been a powerful force in the military mentality, and, through this mentality, upon the Japanese nation at large.

V

Motivating Forces

WHAT were the forces which led Japan to revert to a policy of expansionism in the nineteenth century? Behind the renascent imperialism lay partly a peculiar national psychology of which the characteristics were a sort of inferiority-superiority complex and a resultant sense of mission.

"Viewed in the light of its historical precedents and character and also in the light of its cultural mission," declares Mr. Tatsuo Kawai, former Minister to Australia, and one of Japan's rising diplomats, "expansion on the continent is the destiny of our race." A Marxist, he suggests, might dismiss it simply as a manifestation of monopolistic capitalism in its final stage but the insight of the statesman perceives that "Japan's advance on the continent is partly a racial movement, brought about by the operation of *Musubi,* and only in the light of this fact can Japan's role in the China Affair be properly understood and appreciated." [1]

Mr. Kawai devotes a whole chapter of his book, *The Goal of Japanese Expansion,* to an explanation of *Musubi* as the cosmic principle which brings abundance to life and magnifies truth and beauty. "As children of the gods," he says, "our ancients lived in harmony with nature, acquiring a free and liberal social outlook which has developed into the ideal of universal brotherhood ('the world, one household'). At the same time, perceiving in the forces of nature the operation of a mysterious power, they formulated the philosophy of *Musubi*. This philosophical concept is not a product of any single mind, and it has no formula or system. It is a belief which evolved from the experience of the race.

". . . . From the beginning of their history the Japanese people, as children of nature, pure and innocent, simple and unsophisticated, have constantly practiced the doctrine of *Musubi*. They have grown by negation of self and through fusion and synthesis. The China Affair will after all prove an occasion for the birth of a new life through the operation of *Musubi*."

Japan has no intention of demanding abject submission from China, declares Mr. Kawai, conveniently ignoring Prince Konoye's declaration in 1937 that "we must beat China to her knees." It is all, he explains, a matter of *Musubi:*

"To conform to the Asiatic ideal and to let Japan and China each manifest and magnify their true individual selves within the Asiatic system—that is to practice the philosophy of *Musubi*. Following the dictate of *Musubi*, Japan, together with a resurrected China, will identify herself with the cosmic force that creates and fosters life and will help to promote its endless process in the beautification and sublimation of Asiatic life. Herein lies the foundation of Japan's China policy."

SENSE OF DESTINY

There can be no doubt that from the days of Hideyoshi, who himself was inspired by a strong personal conviction that fate had marked him out for the creation of a Japanese empire overseas, Japanese political thought has been greatly influenced by a sense of predestination. For 200 years prior to 1852, points out Iichiro Tokutomi in his biographical study of Shoin Yoshida, the scholars of Mito had been lecturing "minutely and clearly on the relation of Emperor and *shogun*, the Japanese and foreigners, and the reason for the divine mission of divine Japan *(Jinshu no jinshu yuen)*."[2]

Fanatical belief in the unique superiority of the Japanese state, and hence in its divine mission, emerges from the writings of the leaders of the eighteenth-century Shinto revivial, which, postulating the divine origin of the *Yamato* race, was essentially a movement of self-assertion against the inroads of Chinese culture. These teachings, transmitted in later times by Shoin Yoshida and his circle, are clearly the source from which a good deal of present-day political philosophy in Japan is derived.

By proclaiming this idea of the State, Tokutomi points out, Yoshida "stirred up the hearts of the men of the nation, and united the national sentiment to the extent of opposing foreign countries. His ideas of the State were not the arguments of a scholar of the ancient classics, but the policy, into which he put his blood and his life and his living energy *(katsu ryoku)*, was to awaken the people of his own day from their long night of sleep of the past 300 years and cause them to consent to the good in the new."[3]

Echoes of Shoin Yoshida's fanaticism are to be found in such passages as the following, extracted from a pamphlet issued in 1935 by Major-General Hayao Tada, then in command of the Japanese forces in North China:

"Let us observe the international situation that is changing before our eyes. The progressive change in the international situation may be regarded as a movement against the tyranny and high-handedness of the white people. It may be regarded as the beginning of a racial war for emancipating the colored people, who form the greater part of the human inhabitants of the world, from the enslaving oppression by the whites and realizing equality and peace for all the human beings on earth. It may also be regarded as the beginning of a spiritual war for rectifying the material civilization of the West by the moral civilization of the East.

"These two great missions from Heaven are the natural obligations which our Japanese Empire must bear. Japan has already taken the initial step towards the fulfillment of the obligations by assisting the new State of Manchukuo, withdrawing from the League of Nations and abrogating the Washington Naval Treaty.

"In order to fulfill the great missions imposed by Heaven, our Japanese Empire must keep herself strong and upright. For, it will be impossible for her to care for others if she herself is weak and perpetual expansion of her nation will be impossible if she does not properly employ the strength she has."[4]

Similar sentiments were voiced by Lieut.-General Kenji Doihara in an article published in the *Chuo*

Koron, or *Central Review*, Tokyo, in November, 1938, in the course of which he said:

". . . . It is in the hope of relieving the Orient from this world state of disorder and confusion and thereby contributing to a new world peace and order that Japan engaged herself in the Manchurian Incident and now in the China Incident. Of all the nations in the Orient, Japan alone can be found capable of carrying out this mission with responsibility. Because it is she that has best assimilated the modern world culture, it is neither India, nor China but Japan herself that is preserving as the essential elements of her national life the cream of Oriental civilization, the Buddhist culture of India and the Confucian culture of China." [5]

Even Japanese Christian leaders have adopted this attitude of superiority. "Christianity will prosper," wrote Professor Hiyane, Professor of Comparative Religions at Aoyama Gakuin Theological School, "because we believers are citizens of Japan. . . . In being conscious that we are Japanese subjects we render a great service to Christianity, and at the same time strengthen our faith. . . . Perhaps it is not a dream to hope that we Japanese may be able to propagate and preach the Gospel to the world more vigorously than others, in the same way that we did Buddhism and Confucianism. Our obligations towards Christianity are great; whereas the Christians of other nations have in their recording of history marked the commas, we Japanese Christians must now as a final touch write the period." [6]

"PARANOIA NIPPONICA"

Chosen at random from a large collection of similar Japanese statements,[7] these bombastic declarations point to the survival in present-day Japan of the feeling of cultural inferiority that embittered the eighteenth-century scholars. There is still a clamant urge towards self-assertion and an overweening desire to establish, if necessary at the bayonet point, the imagined superiority of the Japanese race.

In recent years the trend of Japanese thinking and writing has been almost exclusively in the direction of Japonization as against Westernization. Japanese history and tradition, points out Dr. Charles Iglehart in the *Japan Christian Yearbook* for 1941, have been "idealized almost beyond recognition. The classical literature, with its heroes and events in the early mists of semi-historic times, has been diligently searched for application to the requirements of modern Japan. A striking example of this is the re-discovery of the phrase *Hakko Ichiu.* About a year ago it was quoted in an article as having been recorded in the early literature as on the lips of the first ruler of Japan when he ascended the throne. As he set out to quell the disturbances of the unsettled natives who roved along the undefined borders of his domain in central Japan he is said to have promised to bring about a condition of *Hakko Ichiu.*"

Within a few months the phrase was weaving itself into the literature of the nation. It was identified with the real intention of the "New Order in East Asia," which thus obtained a momentum of twenty-six centuries of prestige. Before the Diet, Premier Yonai explained that this principle meant "making the boundless virtues of the Emperor prevail throughout the world." When Foreign Minister Matsuoka went to Russia, Germany and Italy in the interests of further affiliation with these powers he used the *Hakko Ichiu* formula as his text. The term has now come to be accepted as meaning world brotherhood, Dr. Iglehart states, and as having meant that from the beginning.

That the *Hakko Ichiu* concept also worked its way into Christian teaching in Japan is evidenced by the following translated extract from an article contributed by the General Secretary of the National Christian Council of Japan to that organization's *Bulletin* in the summer of 1939:

"What, then, is the plan for the establishment of East Asia? Its purpose is that of realizing the vision emblazoned on the banner of 'the whole world one family' and that purpose, we must recognize afresh, coincides spontaneously with the fundamental faith of Christianity. The policy of extending even to the continent our family principle that finds its centre in an imperial house so that it may bathe in its holy benevolence—this policy, can we not see, is none other than the concrete realization on the earth of the spiritual family principle of Christianity which looks up to God as the Father of mankind and regards mankind as brethren. This is the Christian conception of the Kingdom of God. The basis of the Japanese spirit also consists in this and thus, wonderful to relate, it is one with Christianity. Nay, this must indeed be the great way of heaven and earth. Let us venture to uphold the Christian ideal so that the so-called New Order virtually should become synonymous with the idealism of the Kingdom of God on earth. . . ."[7]

The consciousness that theirs is a borrowed civilization, even though the borrowing was voluntary and spontaneous, has had important effects upon the Japanese mentality and upon the Japanese attitude to the outside world. Seeking psychological relief for a smarting sense of inferiority, they have been led to make extravagant claims for the *Yamato* race and culture as being unique, indigenous and superior to all others.

JAPAN'S WOUNDED EGO

This peculiar mental state of the Japanese has been thus diagnosed by a Chinese writer, Dr. Mousheng Hsitien Lin: "It appears therefore that the Japanese mind suffers severely from these two morbid afflictions —the hypertrophy of the national ego and the complex of national insecurity and inferiority—which not merely exist side by side, but dialectically aggravate each other, thereby generating a poisonous perversion—the will-to-power perversion—which constitutes the core of a systematical delusional state that may be tentatively called *Paranoia Nipponica*."[8]

"The crux of the matter," Dr. Lin goes on to suggest, "is that the Japanese nation, having been overwhelmingly influenced and overshadowed by the Chinese, is deeply wounded—perhaps more unconsciously than consciously—and must struggle to redeem itself, to guarantee its own security, to insure its own superiority. And what thought is more assuring than the divine origin of the *Yamato* race! As the Japanese are divine, all other people are merely mortal."

Because of this inferiority complex the Japanese not only seek solace in highfalutin pretensions, but they are inclined to be supersensitive where questions of national prestige are concerned. The Japanese ego was deeply injured by the rejection of Japan's demand for racial equality at the Versailles Conference and the feeling of bitterness was increased by the passage of the American Immigration Law of 1924 drastically restricting the admission of Japanese into the United States. After the passing of the law fifteen Tokyo newspapers published a joint declaration calling the bill "inequitable and unjust." The jingoist *Yorodzu* declared that America "has pounced upon us with drawn sword and we must defend our honor and interest." In the view of the Tokyo *Nichi Nichi*, Japanese honor had been "mercilessly destroyed," while the chauvinistic magazine, *Japan and the Japanese*, said that the "selfish and arrogant" exclusion of the colored people from the United States would engender great antipathy between the white and colored races. Anti-American demonstrations took place in some Japanese cities, one of which was occasioned by the suicide of a Japanese on account of the exclusion law.[9]

In passing it may be noted that the United States immigration laws bear much more heavily upon the Chinese, who were singled out in 1904 for still more rigid exclusion. According to existing laws, Chinese may enter the United States only at certain designated ports and the Chinese Government is obliged to provide a special certificate, in addition to a passport, for any Chinese who intends to make a temporary visit. This latter provision, Dr. Charles Nelson Spinks points out in an article on the subject in the February, 1942, issue of *Asia*, "is fully tantamount to not recognizing the sovereign power" of China. The Chinese have felt the sting of racial insult just as keenly and have protested against these discriminatory measures from time to time but, unlike the Japanese, they have not allowed it to embitter their relations with the United States.

TERRITORIAL INSECURITY

Despite her geographical isolation both from the Asiatic continent and from the Western world, or perhaps because of it, Japan has developed an ever-increasing sense of national insecurity and consequently has always tended to maintain a sort of defensive-offensive relationship to the outside world. Fear of a strong and unified China has played an important part in conditioning Japan's international policy since the latter part of the nineteenth century.

It must be remembered that Japanese strategy formerly took into account the fact that China, though much weakened by internal rebellion and border troubles, was yet an empire of enormous resources which then, as now, possessed great powers of recuperation. It was considered essential to the Japanese future in Korea that Japanese troops should have free access to Korea at any time, and this access could be rendered certain under all conditions only by the establishment of a maritime superiority over China. Hence after the Japanese victory at Pengyang had removed the last vestige of Chinese influence in Korea the Sino-Japanese war of 1894 was carried to its second phase, culminating in the occupation of Port Arthur and Weihaiwei—the two harbors most likely to be used by China as a naval base.

The creation of a hegemony in Korea was not, of course, the sole motive which led the Japanese to embark upon their first major overseas adventure since the days of Hideyoshi. A desire to resolve the bitter political controversy that had arisen with the introduction of the parliamentary system was coupled with an intention to impress the Western world with Japan's growing importance in the international scheme of things. At this time Japan was engaged in negotiations with Great Britain and the United States for the relinquishment of extraterritorial rights. Japan's leaders—still the young men who had sat at the feet of Shoin Yoshida—believed that the time had come when the nation should demonstrate to the world that she was ready to take her place among the nations of the West. A war with China suited this purpose and, in the event, paved the way to further territorial expansion. When finally China was forced to sue for peace she agreed to cede Formosa and the southern part of Manchuria to Japan in addition to recognizing the independence of Korea.

Japan was robbed of the most valuable fruits of the campaign when Russia persuaded France and Germany to join her in forcing the conquerors to surrender their new territorial acquisitions in return for a cash indemnity of 230,000,000 silver taels. In the eyes of Tokyo, Russia now replaced China as the potential threat to

Japanese security and from about this time onward Japanese policy began to be dominated by the fear that the Russians might establish in Manchuria, Korea or North China a base from which to invade Japan. In 1904 the Japanese army struck once more and, driving the Russians out of southern Manchuria, took over and expanded the large-scale undertakings upon which Moscow had embarked in that territory.

THE RUSSIAN BOGY

Despite the tremendous changes which came over the Far Eastern scene during the intervening decades, the Russian menace, real or imaginary, still remained a cardinal factor in Japanese foreign policy and military tactics. Important though the Chinese question was for Japan, Russia's increasing strength in the Far East, combined with her propaganda activity, presented a still more vital problem. In addition to constituting a potential threat to Japanese security, this Russian development came to be regarded as a factor conditioning Japan's position in China and, to an even greater degree, her position in Manchuria.

"Incidentally," states Professor Masaharu Anesaki, the well-known Japanese scholar, "one may say that such a thing as the Manchurian Incident was mainly an outburst of nationalist reaction. For the whole nation, especially the nationalists and the army, were troubled about the serious menace of insidious propaganda emanating from the northwest, and the measures taken appeared quite inadequate to cope with the situation. Thus the incident of 1931 was regarded as a measure of self-defense in the sense that it was a counterattack against the vicious permeation of an 'invisible army' into Japan by route of Manchuria and Korea, in addition to political and economic considerations." [10]

Parity with Soviet military strength therefore came to be accepted as essential to Japanese security. "To consolidate our defenses on the Asiatic continent and to assure full protection of our first line in case of war with the U.S.S.R.," declared a pamphlet issued by the Japanese War Office at the end of November, 1935, "it is essential to increase the strength of the Japanese garrison in proportion to the strength of the Soviets. Even if the efficiency of the Japanese army is taken into account, it is needless to reiterate the need for achieving approximate equilibrium with the peacetime strength of the Soviets in the Far East."

With the establishment of the U.S.S.R., first Manchuria, then Inner Mongolia and finally North China came to be regarded as Japan's "first line of defense." Ultimately Japan felt it necessary to attempt the establishment of a hegemony in China proper, or at any rate in the provinces adjacent to Manchukuo—with the result that today she finds herself at war once again with China, the latter this time powerfully aided by the United States, Great Britain and, to some extent, by Soviet Russia as well.

A sense of destiny, heightened by a feeling of both cultural and territorial insecurity, has thus tended to generate in the minds of the Japanese leaders a *Drang nach Westen* which has led to successive attempts to extend control in the direction of the Asiastic mainland. Again and again the social and economic fabric of Japan were strained close to breaking point in the interests of expansion abroad. Only in recent years has it come to be realized to what a degree these continental adventures were at the expense of a sound domestic development which might have paid more satisfactory dividends in the long run.

VI

Economic Maladjustments

JAPANESE territorial expansion began long before the country's economic situation became acute, and for a time it continued to follow roughly the method and ideology laid down by Shoin Yoshida and his school. With the rapid increase of industrialization in the twentieth century, however, it came to be rationalized into such modern forms as "population pressure" and "economic necessity." As the result of sedulous propaganda on the part of Japanese officials and publicists, many of these largely specious presentations won much wider acceptance than they actually merited. They have seldom been so trenchantly "debunked" as by Dr. Alvin Johnson, former President of the American Economic Association, in a recent issue of the New School for Social Research *Bulletin*.

"For three hundred years down to the naval demonstration of Commodore Perry," Dr. Johnson writes, "the population of Japan had remained stationary. Death rates were no doubt higher, but the chief instrument of population control lay in the marriage customs, which dissuaded mating in the absence of the means of support. On the opening of commerce with the outside world the means of support increased, and population increased accordingly. If today population tends to outrun support, this is a matter of inadequate social controls, or, more properly, adverse social controls. For the Japanese statesmen, like the German and the Italian, use every resource of propaganda and regulation to encourage early mating and to stimulate fertility. They need more soldiers to win more territory, that their superior races may fill the earth. And what then?

"The whole argument is a fraud, perpetuated by unscrupulous and ambitious politicians. There are no empty territories for the Japanese to occupy; and indeed, the Japanese population itself does not want to remove to the mainland or the islands of the Indian Ocean. Japanese merchants and speculators do indeed resort to these regions in great numbers. The peasants and workers have no desire to compete with Koreans, Chinese or Javanese on alien soil. There is no possibility whatever of settling the annual increase of one million Japanese anywhere outside of Japan. The development of industry and trade might maintain increasing numbers; but sooner or later the Japanese population must establish a limit for itself.

"For the development of industry and trade Japan was in an enviable position, until the militarists ruined her. She had access to the unlimited natural resources of Siberia, the vast markets of China and the Dutch and British Indies. Over this immense area the Japanese could go anywhere and set up shop, in complete security so long as he remained not a spy but a merchant and conducted himself as a reasonably honest man. Japan already had a co-prosperity sphere. She was steadily absorbing the business developed by the Western nations, being able to undersell them. She can not establish a better co-prosperity sphere by war. All she can win by conquest is the enlargement of the immediate gains of the business man by the plunder of existing resources and the exploitation of a monopoly position. This, however, will not solve the population problem. This can be solved only by a military defeat so severe as to throw the crooked militarists out and to turn the power over to civilian common sense."[1]

IS JAPAN OVERPOPULATED?

Japan, it is true, has a population of 73,000,000 packed into an area less than that of California and far less rich in material resources. The fact that a country has a high ratio of people to the square mile and that large numbers of them are in want does not necessarily prove, however, that it is overpopulated. Otherwise many parts of the world could claim to be at least as overcrowded as Japan. Belgium, for instance, has 270 persons to the square kilometer, Holland 233 and England 188 as compared to Japan's 190. It is less a question of mathematical calculations than of the extent to which available resources are intelligently employed. And here most experts agree that Japan is not making the most of existing opportunities.

To begin with, any claims that new territory is needed as an outlet for emigration are largely discredited by the insignificant dimensions which such emigration has assumed in Formosa, Korea and Manchuria up to the present time. By the acquisition of Manchuria in 1931 Japan almost trebled the area of her empire, yet even Japan itself had not yet been fully settled. While it is doubtless true that parts of the country are greatly overcrowded, there are still sections of the Japanese Empire where there is room for expansion. At a conference of Japanese prefectural governors held in Tokyo in 1932, the year after Japan's invasion of Manchuria, the Governor of Hokkaido, the most northern and most sparsely populated region of Japan proper, complained that the government seemed to have forgotten about the plan to encourage migration to the province of Hokkaido, which is estimated to be capable of accommodating an additional two million persons. Up to 1936 only about 600,000 Japanese had migrated to Korea and less than half that number had settled in Formosa.[2] According to the *Japan-Manchukuo Year Book* for 1941, there were less than half a million Japanese residing in Manchuria at the end of 1937.

INCREASE NOT UNUSUAL

The much publicized Japanese population growth is not considered by students of the question to be unusual. They point out that it is merely a repetition of similar increases in Western nations. "With few exceptions," states a well-known expert on population problems, Professor E. F. Penrose of Stanford University, "recent writers have asserted that the rate of increase of the Japanese population has been and is exceptionally high. A writer who speaks of Japan as '*la terre prolifique et pullulante par excellence*' is expressing a view which is widely held in Western countries. None the less, it is an illusion, and there is nothing in vital statistics to support it. Space will not be taken up here with a detailed statistical analysis of the figures for Japan and those for Western countries, but anyone who will compare the recorded increases in the population of England in the nineteenth century with the recorded increases in the Japanese population since the opening up of the country will see that the rate of increase in Japan has been less rapid than that of England in the earlier stages of industrialization. For example, from 1801 to 1851, the population of England and Wales appears to have increased just 100 percent. From 1851 to 1901, it increased 82 per cent. The population of Japan from 1872 to 1922, according to available statistics, increased by 78 per cent. Since no proper census was taken in the nineteenth century, it is unsafe to place much reliance on the earlier vital statistics for Japan. But the available estimates are very probably under rather than over the mark, and, therefore, when used in comparison with recent data tend to exaggerate the increase. This strengthens the conclusion that there is nothing whatever that is surprising or exceptional about the rate of increase of the Japanese population as compared with increases in Western populations.

"An examination of birth-rate statistics gives no support to the view, widely expressed by Western writers, that the Japanese are an extraordinarily fecund people. The highest birth-rate shown for Japan is under 35 per 1,000."[3]

Several estimates of the possible future population of Japan have been offered by different Japanese scholars, including Dr. O. Inagaki, Mr. M. Inouye, Dr. Y. Shimojo and the late Dr. T. Uyeda. Assuming that the birth and death rates for the period 1920-1931 remained constant, Dr. Uyeda figured that the population would increase approximately by ten millions within 30 years and then probably would make no further advance. He estimated that it would approach stabilization at about 80,000,000 by 1955.

SHARP DECLINE NOTED

Professor Shirosu Nasu, Professor of Agriculture at the Tokyo Imperial University, agrees with Professor Penrose that "the trend of the growth of the Japanese population is no exception to the ordinary course taken by industrial nations in the West. With more urbanization of her people, accompanied by retarded marriage age and a fast declining fecundity rate, the peak of the rapidity of her population growth seems to have already been passed." The most important problem in connection with the Japanese population, Professor Nasu suggests, is "not whether it will keep increasing indefinitely, a general misconception, but is rather how to find employment for some three hundred thousand and more people annually during the course of the next two decades." [4]

So far from being concerned about any excess of population, the Japanese Government has recently taken alarm at the sharp decline in the rate of increase, and early in 1941 the Cabinet approved a program aiming to increase the present 73,000,000 to 100,000,000 by 1960. Commenting on this development, statisticians of the Metropolitan Life Insurance Company pointed out, as quoted by the New York *Times* on January 8, 1942, that "there is an obvious incongruity in a national policy that demands more room for excess population at the same time that it urges its people to reproduce more abundantly. There certainly cannot be much sympathy for an illogical program that offers bonuses and all kinds of bribes to the average family to breed more freely while on the other hand it claims that excess population is justification for its territorial robberies."

A further decline in the rate of increase is to be expected, according to the *Economic Survey of the Pacific Area* just issued by the International Secretariat of the Institute of Pacific Relations, and it may well be said "that the capacity of the Japanese people to maintain their growing industries is, unquestionably, very limited, so much so that the rate of industrial expansion since the early thirties has only been maintained at the expense of depleting the rural labor supply." [5]

RAW MATERIAL QUESTION

Why, then, is so much heard about the Japanese "population problem"?

The explanation lies partly in the fact that, just as Japan's foreign policy has been dominated by a morbid fear of attack from outside, her economic program has been influenced, in its larger aspects, by similar considerations. In 1931 the Japanese Foreign Office sought to defend Japan's Manchurian occupation to the League of Nations in the following terms:

"Frankly, it is not unreasonable for us to entertain a

fear as to whether advanced industrial countries will long continue to supply the materials to our industries which compete with their own." [6]

There were apprehensions that the world economic system might be consolidated into large *blocs* from which Japan was excluded. Japan was afraid that one day she might be cut off from the foreign sources to which she looked for the supply of raw materials. This feeling was not appreciably lessened by the fact that she owned iron and coal mines in China and Manchuria, iron mines in Malaya, and rubber plantations in Southeastern Asia, or by the fact that in case of war her fleet would most probably be able to protect many of her trade routes.

Japan was afraid also that she might find herself excluded from world markets. "Countries suffering economic stagnation and anxiety concerning the international situation are jealous of the Empire's foreign trade expansion and her growing political power," declared a propaganda pamphlet issued by the Japanese Ministry of War. "For this reason these countries have introduced all sorts of measures to curtail Japan's economic and political progress. If nothing is done to counteract these measures, Japanese goods will be driven from foreign markets and Japanese emigrants will find closed doors everywhere; politically the Empire will be hopelessly isolated, and it is possible that it will be forced to submit to a destiny similar to that of Germany." [7]

To what exent were the Japanese fears justified?

Examining first the raw materials situation, it is difficult to discover evidence that Japan was in any serious danger of deprivation so long as she behaved herself. Raw materials continued to be shipped to her even after it had become clear that she was cutting down on her output of consumption goods and using these supplies for the manufacture of munitions. Despite tremendous pressure on the part of public opinion, it was not until 1940 that the United States Government moved to impose any important restrictions upon the sale of war materials to Japan. Up to that time the Japanese had been obtaining about 90 per cent of their essential war supplies from the United States, the British Empire, and the Dutch East Indies—the three groups who felt themselves (and rightly as it has turned out) to be next on the list for invasion by Japan's armed forces.

TRADE EXPANDS DESPITE RESTRICTIONS

In the matter of trade restrictions, it is true that from about 1934 onward, as an increasing tide of Japanese exports flowed into world markets which were contracting owing to the depression and other causes, special measures were taken by many governments with a view to limiting the volume of the stream. As the Japanese strained every nerve to dominate the markets of the world, Great Britain, finding herself squeezed out of the Balkans and other European markets, imposed quotas upon the importation of Japanese cotton and rayon piece goods into various parts of the British Empire. Similar action was taken by India, the Netherlands East Indies, the Philippines and Australia.

But these restrictions were imposed less from any political considerations than from a desire to protect home industry against a disruption which would have led to serious unemployment. The need for Japan to expand her exports is understood and accepted. Objection was not taken, it was pointed out at the Yosemite Conference of the Institute of Pacific Relations, "to competition as such but rather to the uncontrolled and disturbing manner in which it was allowed to make itself felt and to the unprecedented (and apparently unwarranted) speed at which Japanese exporters were dislocating western channels of trade." [8]

In her study of Japanese trade expansion Miriam Farley states that during the 1932-37 boom "Japan's industries were actually absorbing considerably more than the natural increase in the labor force (starting, of course, from a basis of severe underemployment) and that any failure to maintain internal economic stability during this period cannot be ascribed primarily to foreign trade restrictions; secondly, that given a proper internal adjustment, a less headlong rate of advance in production and exports would satisfy the needs of the expanding population; and thirdly, that export expansion pursued at a somewhat more moderate rate than that of the immediate prewar years, and controlled to avoid excessive periodic booms and slumps, could be absorbed by world markets without undue dislocation, under conditions of an expanding world economy.

". . . . No small part of the market dislocations and losses occasioned by Japan's recent trade gains has been due to the excessive speed with which Japanese goods, in some cases, practically swamped local markets abroad. Thus a shift which might have taken place with comparative smoothness had it been spread over a longer period proved a source of serious hardship when concentrated with a few short years. . . ."[9]

Despite the restrictions with which they had to contend, however, Japanese exports were able to make headway at a phenomenal rate. After the world depression of 1929 they rose from 1,470,000,000 yen in 1930 to 2,172,000,000 yen in 1934 and to 3,175,000,000 yen in 1937. The increase was most marked in the case of cotton tissues, which expanded from 198,700,000 yen in 1931 to 483,600,000 yen in 1936. By the middle of 1932, Japan had definitely established herself as the world's largest exporter of cotton tissues, and in 1933 she shipped abroad 2,087,000,000 square yards to Great Britain's 2,031,000,000. Between 1929 and 1936 exports to Australia rose from 44,100,000 yen to 68,800,000 yen, exports to India from 198,100,000 yen to 259,100,000 yen and exports to the Netherlands East Indies from 87,100,000 yen to 129,500,000 yen.[10]

This recovery, states an authoritative survey issued in 1940, "was characterized by a great increase in industrial products and employment, and an equally striking increase in foreign trade. Measured by these indices, recovery was probably more rapid and more extensive than in any other industrial country in the world. From the low point of the depression in 1931 to the outbreak of the China Incident in July, 1937, the volume of output more than doubled, industrial employment rose by 60 per cent, and the volume of foreign trade doubled. Because of the depreciation of the currency, the year value of imports and exports showed a much greater gain."[11]

DISTORTED INDUSTRIALIZATION

Since July, 1937, however, as Professor G. C. Allen has pointed out in discussing recent developments in Japanese industry, the industrial structure of Japan has become seriously distorted.[12] In recent years the development of the Japanese industrial system has been determined almost entirely by strategic and military considerations and there has been a shift from light to heavy industry that has proved detrimental to the export trade upon which Japan's prosperity is so largely dependent. Japan's failure to apply her resources along the lines of greatest advantage has proved ruinous to the small and medium-sized establishments which make up the greater part of Japanese industry.

This maladjustment has caused widespread poverty and hence the *appearance* of overpopulation. Whereas in the United States, Great Britain and other industrial countries the main purpose of industry has been to produce consumers' goods in order to make a profit, Japan has industrialized herself primarily for military purposes. The modernization of Japan was, and continues to be, a state policy to increase the nation's power. "Although the Japanese population has doubled," points out Roswell G. Townsend in a careful study of the question, "the welfare of the average Japanese has remained much the same because the inspiration of industrialization is not to sell to the Japanese people but to produce a strong military machine. Wages are kept at a subsistence level while the god of Mars is well fed." [13]

Japan has pursued a militaristic policy which has resulted in widespread poverty, whereas the logical development of light industries, in view of her lack of coal and iron for the establishment of a profitable heavy industry, would have gone far towards supporting her population adequately. Unfortunately, the trend has long been in the opposite direction, and during the past decade Japan has steadily moved towards a totalitarian economy under military direction. When the export trade was subordinated to the overriding claims of military strength peacetime industries steadily declined. Since guns and battleships do not sustain life, this meant poverty for the Japanese masses.

It is clear not only that most of Japan's economic and social difficulties are of her own making, but that attempts to solve them by pursuing a policy of aggression have merely intensified the internal pressure. During the last few decades, it is true, population pressure has had an indirect effect in exacerbating Japan's internal economic problems and she has redoubled her efforts to find a solution for them at the expense of other people rather than by internal readjustments. But, to quote Professor Westel W. Willoughby, "the misfortunes or needs of one State give to it no ethical or moral right to violate the rights of another State, any more than they justify, in private law, the seizure by one individual of another individual's property." [14]

WHAT MIGHT HAVE BEEN

Japan had two possible ways out. The first involved measures for the readjustment of her internal economy, the cultivation of good will and improved trade relations abroad, and a program of international co-operation for checking the rising costs of her raw materials and for developing new sources. Already she had captured most of the trade with China formerly enjoyed by Britain, the United States and other countries. "On the basis of the Chinese Customs returns for the last three years," Mr. Sadao Saburi, a leading Japanese trade expert, told a London audience in March, 1929, "Japan's share of China's foreign trade (imports and exports) amounts to between 30 and 31 per cent, America's share being between 15 and 17 per cent, and Great Britain's averaging 8 per cent. Japan's share is, therefore, about double that of the United States and more than three times that of Great Britain." [15]

During the years immediately preceding the Japanese invasion of Manchuria, Japan's trade in North China was on the increase. "Had Japan followed the advice of its Chamber of Commerce in Shanghai and pursued a policy of friendly cooperation," points out Mr. Julean Arnold, formerly United States Commercial Attache in China, "it is patent that the Chinese were prepared to accord Japanese trading, industrial and financial interests opportunities equally as good as those accorded other foreign nations. For instance, the Chinese Government expressed a willingness to negotiate credit loan agreements with the Japanese for railroad construction on terms similar to those offered other foreign nations. However, Japan's military overlords demanded a degree of supervision over the construction and operation of these lines, which was repugnant to an independent China naturally set upon the preservation of its territorial integrity and sovereign rights.

"Furthermore, it is more than probable that if Japan had been prepared to play the game on the basis of a recognition of the policy of the Open Door, American financiers and manufacturers would have been willing to participate with the Japanese in development projects in China. In fact, Japan with its close geographical proximity to China and its natural facilities for tapping the Chinese markets, stood to gain by everything which other foreign interests might have done towards stimulating the vast modernization program upon which China has embarked."[16]

Japan might have gained all, and more than all, that she would get by war if she had contented herself with trading upon peaceful terms with those countries where proximity gave a specially favorable position. The alternative involved the use of force in order to insure Japanese dominance in Asia—the will-o'-the-wisp of economic self-sufficiency by the path of military aggression. Japan chose that alternative—with consequences that can hardly fail in the long run to prove catastrophical from the standpoint of her future as a major world power.

VII

Nipponism and Nazism

THERE are many points of similarity between the Japanese and Nazi mentalities and methods. As has been shown earlier, the Japanese ruling classes adopted centuries ago the process of mass regimentation which Hitler began much more recently. They discovered that the people, by and large, were stupid and gullible and they proceeded to exploit them to the limit for the sake of conserving and extending their own power. Successive generations of Japanese have been brought up to believe that to live, and, still better, to die for the Mikado is the very essence and end of life. Substitute "State" for "Emperor," and *Yamato Damashii*, or the Spirit of Japan, becomes almost indistinguishable from the Nazi creed with its insistence upon the subordination of the individual in the interest of national advancement.

"From 1615 or thereabouts," points out Sir George Sansom, widely accepted as a leading authority on Japan, "Japan was ruled by a feudal oligarchy, which anticipated in many respects the methods of government used by modern totalitarian states. The distinguishing features were there—the rule of a self-constituted *elite*, the disabilities imposed upon certain classes, the restriction of personal liberty, the sumptuary laws, the monopolies, the censorship, the secret police, and the doctrine that the individual exists for the State. When in 1868 this regime was overthrown it was replaced not by a popular government but by a powerful bureaucracy which—with the adaptations made necessary by Japan's entry into the modern world of international commerce and industry—perpetuated the essential features of totalitarianism."[1]

Ample support for this interpretation of Japanese history is available from Japanese sources. "The ruling class of lords and warriors, being wholly unproductive themselves," says Shunjii Toyama, a Japanese writer now living in America who was formerly a government official, "early recognized the positive necessity for a loyal, contented, and economical working population. To this end they legislated, sermonized, and persecuted unceasingly. . . .

"An accurate gauge of the degree and success of this mass regimentation can be found in the fantastic sumptuary laws that were enforced. A brief mention of a few of the myriad of regulatory measures is enough to make us respect the efficacy of those antique methods of propaganda and control. For it can be said in literal truth that the life of the Japanese was minutely defined and regulated from birth to death. There were laws governing the number and kinds of presents that could be given at childbirth, the toys that could be given to a child, the material and color of clothing worn, the type and quantity of food consumed, the appearance and style of dwellings, the articles of furniture that could be used, the cost of weddings and festivals, the quality of ornaments worn, and the very manner of burial." [2]

Japanese political and military leaders today have "inherited largely through tradition," Toyama goes on to point out, "what the less fortunate dictators in other parts of the world must yet acquire through 'ministers of public enlightenment' and by concentration camps. These modern despots of Europe might well envy the calm patience with which the populace of Japan accept deprivation of their liberties and the never-ending demand for their life and blood. Here, indeed, is a race of men who have forgotten how to 'reason why' but can only 'do or die.'"

TOTALITARIANISM ACCLAIMED

Still more authoritative confirmation is forthcoming from Mr. Toshio Shiratori, formerly Japanese Ambassador to Rome and a vigorous proponent of the Rome-Berlin-Tokyo pact. In the course of an article discussing the principal points of difference between democracy and facism, Mr. Shiratori wrote in 1938:

"In Japan also the tide has turned against that liberalism and democracy that once swept over the nation. The once widely accepted theory of government which sees in parliament the real center of power has now been completely rejected and the country is fast reverting to totalitarianism, which has been the fundamental principle of Japan's national life for the past thirty centuries."

Likening the totalitarian state or nation to one large

tree of which individuals constituted the branches and leaves, Mr. Shiratori said:

"A branch, or a leaf, has its own functions and has, within the whole, its own being and signification. However, it cannot live apart from the whole and must always and willingly sacrifice itself if necessary for the sake of the whole. Such is the political philosophy on which the new state systems of Germany and Italy are based, and such also have been the basic principles of the national system of Japan for millenniums past. The principle is not likely to perish in Germany or Italy whatever may be the fortunes of new statesmen. Japan has had no other principle than this ever since the beginning of her history, although there have been certain external modifications in the governmental form under the influence of political thought imported from abroad. This totalitarian national principle—or national polity, as it is called—is to the Japanese people a thing eternal and immutable. So they feel, and so they believe. No external pressure, no amount of criticism can ever shake this national faith of Japan."

"The national polity of Japan and the spirit of that Oriental culture of which she represents the highest peak are in consonance with the totalitarian principles," he declared. "Accordingly, for Oriental nations, the question is not one of making a new choice but of rediscovering this and returning to their ancient faith. It is a marvel of the present century that Germany and Italy have created a fresh totalitarian formula of government for themselves. It is possible that this formula ideologically may be traced to the ancient philosophy of the Oriental. Be that as it may, it makes our hearts warm to see ideas that have influenced our races for centuries in the past embodied in the systems of these modern states of Europe. . . ."

Equal enthusiasm was voiced in 1938 by another Japanese diplomat, Mr. Tatsuo Kawai, formerly Minister to Australia, in his book, *The Goal of Japanese Expansion*. "In Europe," says Mr. Kawai, "the forces of destruction operating from the eastern sector will be defeated under the salutary influence of the Berlin-Rome Axis. When Europe agrees upon a policy that will allow virile nations, such as Germany and Italy, access to raw materials and markets and enables them to find adequate financial facilities with a view to safeguarding and advancing European peace and civilization, there is not the slightest doubt as to the early and triumphant inauguration of a European system. The world will rest secure on the tripod of these politico-cultural regional groups in America, Europe and Asia, each group endeavoring to promote peace and economic welfare in its own sphere and develop its own peculiar civilization and culture. And then, when mutual and co-operative relations are cultivated among these three groups, we may hope to banish in the end the tragedy of war from the face of the earth. The tripartite division of the world is thus only an antecedent to the unitary evolution and progress of mankind." [3]

NATIONAL MOBILIZATION

The Japanese army has taken the lead in promoting a Japonified national socialist doctrine, but totalitarian ways of thought have for years past been making headway in other branches of government. They have strong adherents in the Departments of the Interior and of Education, while a planned and controlled economy was originated in the Department of Commerce shortly after the Manchurian adventure of 1931. Sir George Sansom, who, as Commercial Counsellor attached to the British Embassy in Tokyo, had unrivaled opportunities for close observation and study over a long period of years, feels it is fair to say that for the best part of a decade the most active, if not the most numerous, elements in the Japanese bureaucracy have been consciously building up a totalitarian system.

Official endorsement was given to these developments by Prince Fumimaro Konoye, then Prime Minister, in his speech at the first session of the "Preparatory Committee for the New National Structure" on August 28, 1940. "The aim of the new national structure," Prince Konoye said, "is to unite the total energies of the State and of the people, to make one living whole of our hundred million countrymen and enable them to fulfill perfectly their duty as subjects of the throne. . . .

"The new national structure movement aims at superseding the old party politics postulated upon liberalism. It is essentially national, all-embracing and public-spirited in character. It aims at the concentration and unification of the nation's entire powers. Its activities extend over the whole life of the nation. Even were this movement to rise as a popular movement, its character would not be that of a political party in the old sense. It would on the contrary be a national movement standing above any political party, embracing all parties and factions, economic and cultural bodies, and uniting all in the spirit of public service. When such a movement is led by the Government itself, it cannot, in any sense, be a party movement. Those who hold the reins of Government and are entrusted with the task of assisting the Throne, are always placed in a position where they must seek the welfare of the whole but never be permitted to indulge in party politics, which, in their very nature, contain elements of sectional antagonism and conflict." [4]

SOCIAL LIFE SUPERVISED

Neighborhood associations (*tonari-gumi*), formerly a feature of primitive community life in Japan, have been revived for the purpose of furthering the national mobilization and bringing about a more coherent discipline in Japanese society. Adjacent households, varying in numbers from two or three to several hundred, but usually about a score, are organized in groups with a government-appointed group leader who is held responsible for the welfare of all the households in his circle. The group leader issues tickets for the distribution of food, fuel and other controlled commodities. He also reports on the progress of the group in national service, and, if need be, in its corporate thinking and attitudes. "Anyone can see at a glance what a serviceable instrument of regimentation such an organization may become, and how its successful development will narrow the area of freedom of its members," comments Dr. Charles Iglehart in the *Japan Christian Yearbook* for 1941.

As in Germany, special efforts have been made to bring religious organizations into line with national requirements. Article XXVIII of the Constitution of the Japanese Empire declares that "Japanese subjects shall, within limits, not prejudicial to peace and order, and not antagonistic to their duties as subjects, enjoy freedom of religious belief." This guarantee of religious liberty is carefully restricted, however, and since 1940 its interpretation has been entrusted by the Control of Religions Act to a police bureaucracy deriving its authority from the absolute sovereignty ascribed to the Emperor. The Act recognizes Shinto, Buddhism and Christianity as religions and provides specifically for the protection of their property rights, with privileges in regard to taxation. Sects and denominations may be disbanded, however, at the discretion of the Minister of Education; local temples and churches at the discretion of prefectural governors. Severe disciplinary and punitive measures are provided for failure to comply with the Act itself, and also for teaching that "subverts peace and order" and for conduct "at variance with the duties of the subject."

Once the Act was passed, the bureaucracy went far beyond what was contemplated by the Diet. Hundreds of special provisions were added by the Ministry of Education and, to make the matter still more complicated, each of the fifty odd prefectures began to weave its own web of extra precautionary regulations around the local application of the law. Instead of according the expected recognition to existing religious groups, the authorities compelled them to combine into a single organization and foreigners were eliminated from the new setup. No foreigner was permitted to occupy a position of authority, even in a local church or school. "Freedom from foreign money and foreigner management" became the slogan and by the middle of 1941 fewer than 200 foreign missionaries were left in Japan out of a total of nearly one thousand.

COMMON MYSTICAL BELIEFS

In the case of both countries a sense of mission lies at the root of their national assertiveness. Hitler's ambitions are little more than a modernized version of the centuries-old doctrine of Pan-Germanism described in the following passage of Sir Eyre Crowe's famous memorandum of January 1, 1907:

"The vague and undefined schemes of Teutonic expansion (*die Ausbreitung des deutschen Volkstums*) are but the expression of the deeply rooted feeling that Germany has, by the strength and purity of her national purpose, the fervour of her patriotism, the depth of her religious feeling, the high standard of competency and the perspicuous honesty of her administration, the successful pursuit of every branch of public and scientific activity and the elevated character of her philosophy, art and ethics, established for herself the right to assert the primacy of German national ideals. And as it is an axiom of her political faith that right, in order that it may prevail, must be backed up by force, the transition is easy to the belief that the 'good German sword' which plays so large a part in patriotic speech, is there to solve any difficulties that may be in the way of establishing the reign of those ideals in a Germanized world."[5]

An equally strong sense of predestination finds expression in the writings of such firebrands as General Sadao Araki, former War Minister in Japan and one of the principal architects of the military dictatorship that has largely negated the advance previously made by parliamentary government. In a pamphlet published in 1933, General Araki said:

"Now, to fulfill the vision 'to conquer the world and embrace the universe as our state' so as to pacify Emperor Jimmu's desire 'greatly to nourish and increase' our ambition has been our traditional policy. If the actions of any of the powers are not conducive to our imperialism, our blows shall descend on that power. . . . Our imperial morality, which is the embodiment of the combination of the true spirit of the Japanese state with the great ideals of the Japanese people, must be preached and spread over the whole world. All obstacles standing in the path of this must be resolutely removed even if it is necessary to apply real force."[6]

But this line of thought is by no means limited to military minds. "Japan is the sole nation qualified to convey to the world the blessings of the Way of the Sage-King," wrote Professor Chikao Fujisawa, of the Great Oriental Culture College of Tokyo and member of the Government Research Institute, in 1935, "and on the realization of this ideal mental equilibrium and moral calm will be restored to afflicted humanity. . . ."

The following quotations from Professor Fujisawa's *Japanese and Oriental Political Philosophy* are equally illuminating:

"Chancellor Hitler says in his book *My Strife:* 'A nation's authority must spring from the peoples' unwavering faith in their administrators' ideal management of government and not from their futile debates in the House.' We guess the Japanese State philosophy in which this kind of authority has provisionally been practiced by *Tenno* will in the near future exert a great influence upon the intelligentsia of Europe and America."

"The Sun is a symbol of the Highest Entity as it shines all over the world with absolute fairness and infinitive love. The words 'Nippon,' which literally mean 'the land from which the sun rises,' are full of superior meaning. Nippon's national flag, *Hinomaru*, is the ensign of 'red heart' or 'fiery sincerity,' an emblem of the Highest Entity . . . it alludes to the heavenly mission of Japan to tranquillize the whole world."[7]

The Nazi conception of a German *Herrenvolk* thus has its counterpart in the Japanese belief in the worldwide mission of the "*Yamato* race." Proud of her "peerless polity" based on Shinto fundamentalism, which conceives a world order founded on monarchical and patriarchal principles supported by military might, Japan shares the Nazi belief in power politics. There is an evident resemblance to Nazi ideology in the following statement by former Foreign Minister Yokosuke Matsuoka in a recently published book:

"I firmly believe that the great mission which Heaven has imposed on Japan is to save humanity. In conformity with the great spirit in which Emperor Jimmu founded the empire, Japan should take over the management of the continent on a large scale, propagate *Hakko Ichiu* (literally translated, 'eight corners under one roof,' meaning that all the world is one household) and the way of the Emperor and then extend it all over the world." [8]

GLORIFICATION OF WAR

Germany and Japan are alike in glorifying war as a way of life. "Every human and social activity," declared the organ of the German Army, *Deutsche Wehr*, "is justified only if it helps to prepare for war. The new human being is completely possessed by the thought of war. He must not, cannot, think of anything else." And it was Hitler himself who said: "War is the most natural, the most everyday matter. War is eternal. War is life." [9]

There is little difference between these sentiments and those contained in a Japanese Ministry of War pamphlet which declared in 1934:

"War is the Father of Creation (*Sozo no chichi*) and the Mother of Culture (*Bunkwa no haha*). Rivalry for supremacy does for the state what struggling against adversity does for the individual. It is such impetus, in the one case, as in the other, that prompts the birth and development of Life and Cultural Creation (*Bunkwa-teki sozo*).

"War, in this sense, does not conform to the generally accepted conception, in which it is held to consist of a series of terrific destructive acts perpetrated by massed people for unrelenting slaughter and devastation. War, thus characterized, is simply an inevitable outcome of the application of the idea that 'might makes right,' an insatiable thirst after sheer conquests. Such definition of war must be rejected forthwith by our people, who have an unshakable faith in the all-pervasive Life of the Universe (*Banyu-no-seimei*), and who are animated by the belief that it is their heaven-sent mission to participate in the great work of helping the Life of the Universe to unfold and infinitely to develop. Accordingly, the greatest responsibility imposed upon our Empire is that, on the one hand, of checking all forms of the idea that "might makes right," which naturally stand in the way of our efforts to discharge our great mission in our pursuit of righteousness, and of our creative activities, and, on the other hand, of taming, correcting and directing all evil forces that tend, with baneful will, toward the grasping of power for power's sake. And we must do this in such manner as to cause our endeavors to be transformed into, or to be assimilated with, the benign and magnanimous soul of Japan (*Wakon*) and to flow into that majestic and all-embracing course of universal justice (*Kodo*), or the Imperial Way. To exalt war to such a high level is, in short, the mission of national defense."[10]

According to Mr. Tatsuo Kawai's *The Goal of Japanese Expansion*, the armament of a nation is "a symbol of the nation's tense energy, which may be released in peace time for the ceaseless creation of cultural values. It also embodies the Japanese philosophy of 'the sword that slays not' by forestalling any occasion for resorting to armed force." And in another passage he writes: "War—the unlimited exercise of brute force—can be made the mother of civilization. . . ."[11]

As Hitler has done so successfully in Germany, Japan's military leaders have capitalized on the Japanese strain of ill-defined mysticism—a blind faith fed on phrases about Japan's mission, Japan's destiny, etc., which thrives on blind obedience to blind doctrines. By skillful manipulation, the mental texture of the Japanese people and their deep-rooted religio-nationalism have been woven into a closely knit pattern that blends perfectly with the Nazi system.

NAZI MODELS FOLLOWED

Characteristic again of the totalitarian mind, Japan, like Germany, has complained of "encirclement" every time her intended victims showed any signs of drawing together. She has striven to conceal calculated acts of agression behind a smoke screen of "have-not" propaganda. The German New Order has a close parallel in the "Greater East Asia Co-Prosperity Sphere," which recalls Hideyoshi's proposal in 1578 to conquer Korea and China so that "the three countries, China, Korea and Japan will be one." Several secret societies, notably the Black Dragon Society and the Black Ocean Society, appear to have anticipated them in their propaganda, but theories of self-sufficiency in Japan were partly derived from German sources such as Friedrich Ratzel's *Politische Geographie*, published in 1897.

With the rise of Fascism and Nazism in Europe the totalitarian implications of *Geopolitik* came to be popularized in Japan, where Major-General Karl Haushofer, the Nazi geopolitician, who had served as military attaché in Tokyo in 1908, is credited with having exercised a strong influence upon modern Japanese thought. Haushofer's magazine, *Zeitschrift für Geopolitik*, was eagerly read by Axis-minded Japanese, and Nazi concepts found their way into Japanese literature and official documents. Odious comparisons were drawn between the blitzkrieg speed of Germany's *Grossraumwirtschaft* (Great Space Economy) and the slower tempo of its Japanese counterpart, the effort to establish a Greater East Asia Co-Prosperity Sphere.[12]

The "Nazification" of Japan was greatly accelerated after the conclusion of the Anti-Comintern Pact in 1936. In accordance with the terms of the pact, police officers were exchanged for the purpose of advising on the suppression of Communism, and a representative of the German Gestapo, Herr Franz Huber, was installed in the Home Ministry in Tokyo. The advice offered by Herr Huber and the swarm of Nazi agents by whom he was soon joined went far beyond the provisions of the Anti-Comintern Pact, however. The German Embassy, reported Wilfrid Fleisher, formerly the well-informed Tokyo correspondent of the New York *Herald Tribune*, in a book published in 1941, "advised the Foreign Office as to what German teachers might best be employed in Japanese schools and what German businessmen could be counted upon as dependable, and German military and naval men were helpful in advising the Japanese on matters of strategy in China, where a German military mission had trained the Chinese Nationalist army. . . .

"German Jews employed as professors in Japanese universities or connected with cultural institutions were dropped on the 'advice' of the German Embassy and were replaced by incumbents with official Nazi backing. German teachers, businessmen, tourists and newspapermen have come in increasing numbers within recent years. Whereas in 1936 there were only two or three German correspondents in Tokyo, the Nazi press contingent, now by far the largest, numbers over thirty."[13]

The Japanese thus share with the Nazis far more than a common hatred of the United States and Great Britain. In addition to a natural talent for regimentation they have the same mystical belief in their "destiny" as a super-race, the same determination to establish themselves at the head of a group of slave states. And they have adopted much the same unscrupulous methods to gain their ends. The so-called "New Order" which the Japanese are seeking to establish in Europe is no more compatible with democratic ideals than is Hitler's demand for *Lebensraum* in Europe.

VIII

Conclusion

In the preceding chapters it has been shown that, amid outward changes, the influences of a highly developed feudal mentality have remained strong in Japan, where there exists a totalitarianism of a peculiarly traditional and religious quality. The manner in which the Japanese ruling class rejected the leveling and humanizing influences first of Chinese political philosophy, and subsequently of Western democracy and of Christianity, has been described. It has been demonstrated, too, that ideas of world domination were working in the blood of the Japanese for generations prior to the reopening of the country to foreign intercourse in the middle of the nineteenth century. An analysis of motivating forces behind Japan's expansionist program pointed to the existence of deep-rooted psychological causes and suggested that popular economic explanations were inadequate.

From this it is evident that, postulating an anti-Axis victory, careful thought must be given to the handling of a defeated Japan if the whole disastrous business is not to be repeated at some future stage. Time and caution will be needed before reliance can be placed in any Japanese conversion from tribalism to democratic, peaceful ideas.

"If Germany, after a long and unbroken record of evil-doing, is ever to cease to be a curse to herself and to everyone else," declared Sir Robert Vansittart, formerly Chief Diplomatic Adviser to the British Government, "she will have to undergo the most thorough spiritual cure in history; and part at least of that cure will have to be self-administered. It will have to comprise a complete change of heart, mind and soul; of taste and temperament and habit; a new set of morals and values, a new, a brand-new way of looking at life."[1]

An equally fundamental change will be needed in the case of Japan before we can begin to feel secure. There must be, for one thing, a change-over from power to human welfare as the underlying basis of state policy. The present roles of guns and butter in the Japanese scheme of things must be reversed. Japan's distorted industrial machinery must be rationalized, by the Japanese themselves and for the benefit of the Japanese population, as a condition precedent of outside assistance in the matter of raw materials and of markets. There will thus arise the difficult problem of conveying to the Japanese a real sense of the consequences of defeat and at the same time placing before them a way of readjustment which offers the possibility of transition from one ideology to another.

ROLE OF THE EMPEROR

Many well-informed students of Japanese affairs question whether any permanent change could be effected without some drastic curtailment of the role now fulfilled by the Emperor. They fear that so long as the Mikado retains his mystical hold over the minds of the Japanese people there will always remain the danger of his being used by reactionary groups as a weapon to defeat any attempt at social reconstruction. It is suggested that any peace treaty should insist upon amendment of the Japanese Constitution so as to provide for a real constitutional monarchy in place of the present sham. It is also felt by some that the role which emperor worship plays in Japanese education should be drastically proscribed.

Others more closely acquainted with Japanese conditions find it difficult to visualize the possibility of forcing the Japanese in this fashion to change a national psychology which has its roots so firmly embedded in the past. They suggest that under the sting of defeat there might arise in Japan a good many influential people who would do everything they could to prevent the Emperor's position from being exploited by power-seeking groups. It would be better, they argue, to let the Japanese manage the business in their own way. If outsiders stepped in it might cause a tremendous reaction which would defeat the end in view.

The fact that the Japanese Constitution has never been amended does not mean that it could not be changed. The machinery is there. Just as the document was drafted by a commission, approved by the Privy Council and promulgated by the Emperor, Dr. W. W. McLaren, the well-known Meiji historian, pointed out in a discussion of the subject in 1914,[2] so its emendation would have to be undertaken by a commission whose function would be to draft the necessary changes. That draft would have to be approved by the Privy Council, sanctioned by the Emperor, and finally accepted by the two Houses of the Diet. Apart from amending the Constitution along lines which he outlined in detail, Dr. McLaren emphasized the necessity of rescinding the rule of the Privy Council which prevents a civilian from holding the cabinet offices of Minister for War or Minister for the Navy. The expunging of that rule would of course deprive the two services of their present power to destroy, by the simple process of refusing to participate in it, any government of which they disapprove.

Such changes have been sought by liberal statesmen in Japan, Dr. Charles Brooke Elliott, Assistant Professor of Political Science at Ohio State University, pointed out in a letter published in the New York *Times* on February 15, 1942. "Indeed," Dr. Elliott said, "the demand for them became so great that it helped to goad the military into the *coup d'état* of September, 1931. It will be revived when defeat overseas and on the beaches of Japan sends into oblivion General Tojo's version of the Shogunate.

"In this manner perhaps—but never by a madcap program of violence to their Emperor—shall we set the Japanese people once more upon the road to democracy. This may be the long way around, but it is the only way for the Japanese to take if they are to reach that goal in the foreseeable future."

EFFECT OF DEFEAT

Undoubtedly defeat would be for Japan a tremendously critical experience involving great economic and social strain. In the expectation of many people it would have the result of discrediting the military oligarchy through the failure of its expansionist program. There are important qualifying considerations to be borne in mind, however. There is the possibility that defeat might be rationalized as having been due to unscrupulous machinations on the part of Japan's enemies, to the unforeseeable failure of Axis allies, and at most to an error of judgment on the part of individual military officers. Thus thought might be so clouded that Japan would offer fertile soil for an Oriental version of Hitlerism with revenge as an organizing principle.

The risk may be reduced to some extent by just and tactful treatment on the part of the victors, but if permanent peace is to be established the power of the Japanese military oligarchy, counterparts of the Prussian junker and the Nazi demagogue, must somehow be broken. Only then perhaps will it be possible to bring about anything like an effective democracy in Japan. But it may well be doubted how far this can be achieved by intervention from outside. The job is essentially one for the Japanese people themselves; a mass upheaval may be needed in order to dispose of the feudal regime with any completeness and to smash the bridges leading back to the past.

IS REVOLT POSSIBLE?

What would be the chances of an antimilitarist revolt? It may be instructive to study the views which some well-known Far Eastern experts have expressed on this much debated question.

"The terrible poverty of the Japanese people and the revolutionary ferment amongst all classes, except a small circle of wealthy men, would certainly break out in social revolution," Freda Utley believes, "if Japan suffered even one severe defeat, or found herself involved in a long and costly war, or even if she were faced with economic sanctions. . . . Any major reverse would force open the gates and Japan would be swept off her insecure foundations and submerged in the flood of revolt." [3]

Drawing upon his long experience as a newspaper correspondent in Tokyo, Wilfred Fleisher expresses the opinion that, while there appears to be no possibility of a popular revolution in wartime, an Axis defeat "would be certain to result in a swing back to a policy of moderation, while a defeat of Japan herself, never experienced in Japanese history, might well produce the popular uprising the wishful thinkers abroad have been looking for." [4]

Other observers are more dubious. A military defeat might well contribute to a social revolution, Sir George Sansom declares, but he goes on to point out that we have very little precedent for judging what form such a social revolution would take. "It might include violence and civil disturbance; but it might equally well be achieved by one of those feats of compromise for which the Japanese have a remarkable aptitude. This is all that can be safely predicted at the moment, save that the defeat of totalitarian states in Europe will be more cogent than any other argument in persuading Japan to revise her present principles of government."[5]

Nathaniel Peffer takes a decidely negative view. "One of the commonest questions put here to those returning from Japan is," he writes; "'What are the prospects for Japanese revolt against military domination?' The answer is: None. There will be revolution against the military in Japan when it is no longer necessary; when, that is, the military have been crushed from without—this because the Japanese are what they are.

"There are, no doubt, groups in Japan that do not like the military rulers, but they do not dislike them enough to try to block their actions against non-Japanese. Institutionally, the nation is so organized that they could do nothing if they wanted to. Psychologically, the nation is so constituted, by reason of the past rather than because of biological endowment, that it would not occur to them to try to do anything. The concept that something could or should be tried to frustrate the ruling caste is wholly outside their consciousness."[6]

DEMOCRATIC LEADERSHIP LACKING

Optimists point to the fact that for a few years after the 1914-18 European conflict there was a period during which liberalism appeared to make considerable headway in Japan and the militarists were relegated to a back seat. It must be remembered, however, that at this time Japanese expansionism had been thrown into reverse by a series of economic setbacks, due partly to the postwar depression and partly to the great earthquake of 1923, which placed a great strain upon the mushroom growth of Japanese industry. Backed by the powerful Mitsubishi trading interests, Baron Kijuro Shidehara adopted towards China a policy of friendship in the hope of conserving the important Chinese market. Although Baron Shidehara is entitled to much credit for the courage and persistence with which he advocated conciliation, it was a matter of economic expediency, or enlightened self-interest, rather than a renunciation of aggression so far as the Japanese as a whole were concerned. The reactionary elements were never happy about Shidehara's "weak-kneed policy," as it was termed, and with the fall of the Wakatsuki cabinet in April, 1927, General Giichi Tanaka, reputed author of the famous Tanaka Memorial and an avowed expansionist, was appointed to the premiership. When Baron Shidehara returned to office under Mr. Hamaguchi in 1929 he did his best to counteract the unfortunate affects of the aggressive Tanaka regime but the army continued to agitate for sterner measures and in September, 1931, they plunged the country into hostilities with the occupation of Manchuria. Since then the foreign policy of Japan has been almost exclusively a military affair.

Internally this period was marked by an upsurge of radicalism which has suggested to some observers that the intellectual resources for a political revolution are not lacking in Japan if they are but given a chance. From 1919 onwards professors and other intellectual leaders began to study and discuss publicly the works of Marx and Lenin, and student thought took a distinctly anti-imperialist, antimilitarist turn. A Communist Party was formed in 1922, and numerous other radical groups sprang into existence after the passing of the Universal Suffrage Act in 1925 had swelled the electorate from about three millions to more than four times that number.

The inevitable reaction followed, however, and the Government soon introduced a Peace Preservation Law, supplemented by emergency regulations, under which widespread arrests were made by the police with a view to eliminating these "dangerous thoughts." According to Professor Masaharu Anesaki, the radical movement remained essentially an intellectual one, and scarcely touched the working classes. Its effect, he points out, was to intensify the nationalist reaction, "until it included almost every activity within its scope. There was an increase in the study of the nation's past and in the emphasis laid on the old moral and religious traditions; there was a great encouragement of all movements opposed to 'dangerous thought,' and in the schools and colleges military training was more vigorously enforced, whilst patriotic youth was organized on the lines of the boy scouts. Police and judiciary repression was intensified, and a kind of inquisition office was even established in the department of education. . . ." [7]

On balance, it seems highly doubtful whether, even under conditions of unconditional defeat, there would be sufficient leadership forthcoming in Japan to overthrow the military regime. Democratic organization has had little chance to develop among the Japanese;

such opposition as has existed has been concerned with detail rather than directed against the system as a whole. When the shogunate was displaced in 1868 the rallying point was the Emperor and it simply meant that one oligarchy was replaced by another. There appears still to be no alternative political philosophy around which dissident elements could be organized.

PROBLEM OF SECURITY

The problem is thus an exceedingly difficult and delicate one. Because they have been kept in political fetters for centuries, one is tempted to feel that the Japanese share the responsibility for the actions of their government far less than the people of other countries which have attained a higher state of political development. Nevertheless, although there are some groups and individuals in Japan who may have disliked executing the programs of their military rulers, the fact remains that these programs have invariably been carried out.

It has been said that "the *German* is often a moral creature; the *Germans* never; and it is the *Germans* who count." [8] Perhaps the only safe way will be to view the Japanese in the plural also and to proceed on the assumption that, while the process of democratization can be assisted by wise and intelligent statesmanship on the part of the victors, it may take several generations, during which period Japan will have to be kept under some form of restraint. Military disarmament presumably could be enforced and supervised by some kind of international commission; "psychological disarmament" would perhaps have to be entrusted to the working of time and events.

Meanwhile security would have to be provided in some fashion both for Japan's neighbors and for herself. Japan must not be left with reason to fear an attack from China or Soviet Russia. By the same token, other countries—notably China, Soviet Russia and Australia—would need to be reassured against any recrudescence of Japanese aggression. Some form of international peace-keeping arrangement backed by overwhelming force would be required for this purpose.

THE CHINESE POSITION

The problem of postwar Japan cannot be considered without reference to the probable Chinese attitude and here it may be useful to study views which have recently been put forward by responsible Chinese statesmen. For a reasonable statement of what, in the Chinese estimation, are the prerequisites of peace in the Pacific it is scarcely necessary to look further than the paper read by Dr. Hu Shih, the Chinese Ambassador to the United States, at the annual meeting of the American Political Science Association on December 31, 1941. In that paper Dr. Hu declared that a just and durable peace in the far east must fulfill these basic conditions:

(1) It must not result in vindicating any territorial gain or economic advantage acquired by the use of brutal force in open violation of international law and solemnly pledged treaty obligations.

(2) It must satisfy the legitimate demands of the Chinese people for an independent, unified, and strong national state.

(3) It must restore and greatly strengthen the international order for the Pacific area and in the world at large so that orderly international relationships may always prevail and aggressive wars may not recur.

Dr. Hu explained that in specific application his first point meant, as he saw it, the complete restoration to Chinese sovereignity and government of all the territories of Manchuria, Jehol, Chahar and Suiyuan as well as the occupied parts of North, Central and South China. It also meant, he said, that at the peace conference at the end of the war "the wishes of the twenty-two million people in Korea should be given a fair hearing and just consideration, and steps should be taken to see sovereign rights and self-government restored to these people." (It may be noted as of possible significance in this connection that the revolutionary Provisional Government of the Republic of Korea has established its headquarters in Chungking and that a force of 30,000 Koreans is reported to be co-operating with the Chinese armies.)

Dr. Hu defined "an independent, unified and strong national state of China" as meaning "a sovereign China free from all forms of so-called political and economic 'co-operation and collaboration' which her aggressive neighbor had been forcing upon her." He envisaged, too, a China freed from the remaining legal or extraterritorial restrictions imposed upon her by the other powers in the last century—a China free, in the words of the Nine-Power Treaty, "to develop and maintain for herself an effective and stable government"; a China free, in the words of the Atlantic Charter, "to choose the form of government under which the people will live."

"LEAGUE TO ENFORCE PEACE"

Amplifying his third point, the restoration, strengthening and reinforcing of an international order for the Pacific area, Dr. Hu pointed out that to be effective such a regime must be backed by overwhelming force. "The new world order which we want to see set up as the necessary condition or pre-condition for a durable peace in the Pacific area or in any other part of the world must be," he urged, "a 'League to Enforce Peace'—it must be, in the words of President A. Lawrence Lowell, 'some kind of international organization based upon the principle of a threat of overwhelming power to prevent aggressive war.' This new world order must command a sufficient amount of organized force to support its law and judgment, and thereby to effectively enforce peace. Its provisions for economic and military sanctions against all possible violations of peace and order must be so clear and so unmistakable that no evasion of responsibility will be possible and that both aid to outraged victims and penalty to the aggressors will not be unduly delayed."

Since Dr. Hu Shih is rightly considered a moderate, it may safely be assumed that his views represent the minimum position likely to be taken up by the Chinese at a peace conference. Little information is available as to the views of Chinese leaders in China and it may be doubted perhaps whether, preoccupied as they are with the business of waging war, many of them are giving much thought at present to the question of peace. In his declaration of September 18, 1941, on the eve of the tenth anniversary of the Japanese invasion of Manchuria, however, Generalissimo Chiang Kai-shek made it abundantly clear that he regarded Manchuria as an inalienable part of China's sovereign territory and that Japanese aggression "could not be effectively terminated so long as it drew its sustenance from the rich resources of China's northeastern provinces." This view was endorsed at the second plenary session of the People's Political Council in Chungking the following November.[9]

Other Chinese spokesmen have urged that Japan should not only be disarmed but should be deprived of all footholds (including property, factories, mines, railways, etc.) on the Asiatic mainland, including China proper, Manchuria, and Korea; also that Japan should be ousted from Formosa, the Loochoos, the Kuriles, the Bonins and other insular possessions adjacent to the mainland as well as from the mandated islands. Some would be prepared to see these island territories made available to Britain and America as naval and air bases.

It is felt by the Chinese that, as part of the eventual peace settlement, the slate should be wiped clean so far as Japan's interests and holdings in China are concerned. This does not imply an intention to exclude the Japanese in perpetuity, however. It is simply thought that the only way to put Sino-Japanese relations on to a proper basis is to start again from scratch.

COATING THE PILL

Nothing that falls far short of what has been outlined above is likely to satisfy the Chinese after their prolonged and exhausting war of resistance; yet it would be an enormously bitter pill for Japan to swallow. What sort of sugar-coating might be applied to make the medicine slightly more palatable, at any rate to the more reasonably minded Japanese?

It will be the part of wise statesmanship to make it possible for a genuinely reformed Japan to take her proper place in the comity of nations. Even with the expected check to the extension of her Empire, the propinquity and the character of her manufactures will still leave her with a considerable advantage in East Asia over her competitors. Any proposals for a settlement in the Far East must seek to provide Japan with a full opportunity to exploit these opportunities. She will need to be given reasonable assurances that, as foreshadowed in the Atlantic Charter, she will be able to enjoy "access, on equal terms, to the trade and to the raw materials of the world." In this connection it has been suggested by some thoughtful students of the Far Eastern problem that, of her own volition rather than as a matter of international compulsion, China might go further and declare that for ten years she would give special consideration to Japan as a purchaser, purely on a commercial basis, of such raw materials as China could spare for export. Similar arrangements might perhaps be made by other countries in eastern Asia, thus opening up a clear long-range program of fair opportunities in respect of raw materials and markets on which Japan could base her policies.

Strings must be attached to these gestures, however, if they are to have any permanent value. It must be stipulated that Japan shall do her part by introducing measures of economy, by social reform and particularly by the readjustment of her distorted and ill-balanced economic system. It should be made clear to Japan that she will greatly further the effective recognition by the world of her rightful place in political and economic associations if she proclaims and implements a course that allows her people increased freedom of mind and of expression, and thus prepares them for genuine co-operation with other nations. She should be reminded that the peace, security and welfare of the world require of all countries a respect for their neighbors and a direction of policy that will permit other peoples to go forward without fear of aggression.

Appendix A

GENERAL SHIGERU HONJO'S LETTER TO THE JAPANESE MINISTER OF WAR OUTLINING A PLAN OF WORLD CONQUEST *

Your Excellency, General Jiro Minami, Minister of War:

Having carefully studied the question of perpetuating the national existence of our Empire and consolidating its position as a first-class power, I, S. Honjo, have come to the conclusion that unless we actually occupy Manchuria and Mongolia which we have developed for three decades and attain the object which we had when we despatched a military expedition to certain places in Siberia in the 8th year of Taisho, so as to unite the above places and Korea with our interior as one piece of territory, during this opportune moment when the world is facing an economic depression, when the five-year scheme of Soviet Russia is not yet completed, and when the unification of China is not yet accomplished, we cannot expect to effect the consolidation of the national foundation of our Empire in the present-day conditions of the world. I shall now report in detail the result of my investigations so far made.

The renaissance of China, the continuous existence of "Red" Russia and the eastward advance by the United States on the Pacific Ocean, are all anathemas against the national policy of our Empire. But in order to be able to prevent the eastward advance of American influence, we must first consolidate our national defences on the

---

* *China Critic* (Shanghai) Vol. 4, p. 1183 (December 3, 1931). Also *Documents Illustrative of Japan's National Policy* (Nanking: Council of International Affairs, October 27, 1937), pp. 13-17.

land and attain a position of independence as far as material supplies are concerned. Therefore, before declaring war on America, we must strive to gain a superior position for our military strength both in China and in Russia. We must aim to cripple China and Russia once for all; or in case we should be unable to destroy their power entirely, we must at least reduce them to temporary impotency so that they would not be able for some time to attack us or to regain their feet. Our Empire would thus be enabled to seize hold of vast quantities of rich natural resources in our newly occupied lands. When profitably applied, they could be the means of strengthening our sea defences, and driving the American influence to the east of Hawaii. Then there could be no question at all that the Philippine Islands would fall into our control. We could then be the sole master on the Pacific and nobody would be in a position to compete with us or to make a protest.

Having vanquished the American influence in the East, the British influence in Singapore and Hongkong would not be potent enough to do us any harm; moreover, it would soon be destroyed by our navy also; while the South China Sea would likewise come under our jurisdiction. Thus, all the 400 counties of China would fall into our hands, while the unification of the whole of Asia and the subjugation of Europe would both prove to be tasks quite feasible and not difficult to be carried out. Let us try to state our order of procedure as follows:

Our first step should be to occupy Manchuria and Mongolia of China and make them an independent state of Manchuria and Mongolia.

Our second step would require us to make good use of the Chinese Eastern Railway to attack and penetrate Siberia until we occupied Upper Udinsk and forced Russia to cede to us the great plains east of the Lena River and up to the Behring Strait. We could then help the White Russians and the Buriats to inaugurate an independent state of the Far East. Of course, these two independent states (Manchuria and Mongolia and The Far East) would be ruled and controlled each by a governor-general appointed by Japan. Thus, the Sea of Okhotsk and the Sea of Japan would both be wholly incorporated as part of our Empire, and we would have then to look after its sea defences facing the southeast only.

Should the above-mentioned places fall into our control, their rich resources would, I find, really contribute very materially to making our Empire a first-class power in every sense of the term, whose position as a military power would be impregnable.

I find that Manchuria and Mongolia of China comprise three provinces, namely, Fengtien (Liaoning), Kirin and Heilungkiang and the easternmost part of Inner and Outer Mongolia with an area of over 74,000 square miles, or nearly treble the size of our Island Empire. The large plains east of the Lena River in Russia embrace all the lands in the provinces of Lower Baikal, Yakutsk and Amur as well as the North Sakhalin; and their area is over 300,000 square miles, or more than seven times the area of Japan Proper. The total number of population in these two regions is less than forty millions, only about a half of our own population (including the population of Korea and Formosa). With such an extensive area of territory so sparsely populated in our possession, our Imperial Government need feel no apprehension at all as regards the accommodation for any surplus population for the next two hundred years provided every opportunity to make use of the advantages be availed of.

In addition, the riches in agriculture, mines, forestry, cattle-breeding and fishery there are truly incalculable. Besides, the lengthy rivers and large lakes are also very precious in that the water power they are able to furnish would supply whatever amount of electricity these fertile plains might require. As the fertility of the vast tracts of land along both banks of the Sungari and Nonni rivers and the Liaoho and Heilungkiang is well-known, their development in a skillful way by the engineers of Japan would surely result in the multiplication of their productive quantity, ¾ per cent of which would be ample to make up the deficiency of agricultural products in Japan, while more than 80 per cent could be diverted to meet the requirements of the world markets.

The field for the fishing industry along the coast of the Sea of Okhotsk is counted to be one of the three principal fields in which the fishing industries flourish most in the world. If the industry is developed by the Imperial Japanese Government with all its available resources, the profit to be derived therefrom is estimated to amount to something round about 1,000,000 yen per annum. Even more than this enormous amount will be the profit derivable from hunting whales.

Ponies abound in Chita and Jehol, hides and wool are produced in unlimited quantities in many places. Raw material for making silk fabrics now being imported could be supplied from our own production. Oil mines have, to my knowledge, been found in as many as fifty spots, and the quantity they hold is believed to equal the quantity found in two of the richest oil-bearing provinces. The problem of meeting the fuel requirements of our industries, our navy and aviation service would thus be solved once for all. Gold in large quantities is also embowelled in the earth. China and Russia have opened mines at eight places. During this time of a shortage of gold production, if we would but devote our Empire's energy to an intensive digging for gold our national wealth could be increased a hundredfold.

Coal and iron need not be mentioned. Compared with the poverty-stricken conditions in our interior, these regions appear, indeed, to be the happy land in Heaven. If we make good use of these resources, there can be no limit to the expansion of our industries in the future.

Forest wood is as profusely grown there as in Canada. If our paper manufactures would make advantageous use of this produce, they could control the markets of the world.

If all the above-mentioned places are placed under our administration, our Empire will in less than ten years acquire a wealth exceeding that of the United States of America. When that time arrives, will there be any country in the world which will be found sufficiently powerful to oppose and compete with our Empire?

With such wealth and resources at our disposal, we would encounter not the slightest difficulty even should we elect to train an army twice the size of the armies of China and Russia and to maintain a navy equal in strength to the navies of Great Britain and the United States. We would then be in a position to drive away the United States to the east of Hawaii and Great Britain to the west of Singapore and to hold supreme power on the Pacific without any difficulty. While all the islands constituting the South Sea Archipelago now under Dutch rule as well as the British colonies of Australia, New Zealand, etc., would be within easy grasp at our Imperial will. Once we had attained such an influential position, we could proceed to conquer the whole country of China and the whole continent of Asia, and further to subjugate the whole continent of Europe as well as that of Africa by force until we have gained control of the Eastern Hemisphere of the Globe when we would share equally with the United States (the good things of) this world, in accordance with the instructions contained in the will of our late Emperor Meiji and as becomes the fitting duty that our Taiwa Race (Japanese nation) must carry out.

At present, Russia and China are still in the preliminary stage of the process of their rebirth, that is, they are both still weak in strength. Were we to bring our military pressure to bear upon them now, they could be swept off their feet as easily as the breaking of a rotten log. If we did not act this moment; if we should passively watch the unification of China to become a fait accompli, the execution of Chiang Kai-shek's ambitious program for the reconstruction of China to its logical end, and the completion of the five-year industrial plan by Soviet Russia, not only would the hopes and aspirations which our Empire is looking forward to materialize in the future be all shattered, but a great calamity would, I am afraid, soon befall our Imperial Nation.

I beg to lay before Your Excellency a detailed report, together with sketches and plans, presenting the result of investigations I have made for your consideration. (Plans and sketches not reproduced.)

Appendix B

CHAPTERS FROM GENERAL SADAO ARAKI'S PAMPHLET GIVING HIS CONCEPTION OF THE MISSION OF JAPAN UNDER THE REIGN OF SHOWA *

Chapter 2. To the Entire Japanese Race

1. THE WORLD AND JAPAN

An examination of the position of Japan in the world reveals that since the Restoration (1867-73), while the true bearing of Japan shows all over, she has always been upholding righteousness, not at all unwilling to sacrifice everything for the protection of peace. Yet there are times when she does not hesitate for a moment to use her might to eliminate that which is evil. This is of course due to the sovereign power of His Majesty our heavenly emperor; nevertheless the growing mighty spirit of the people since the Restoration, which has so happily adjusted itself with the turn of events, never for once running against the natural tendencies and bending headlong toward self sacrifice in loyally supporting the imperial plan, has contributed much. By the support of the imperial plan is meant the realization of the great ideal of *Dai Nippon*. To sacrifice themselves for this realization is of course the "great vehicle of self awakening" which the entire Japanese people await and hope for with burning zeal. But recently, this hearty spirit of

* Translated by Mr. Jen Tai from Mr. Liu Wen-Tao's Chinese version published in the *Ta Kung Pao*, May-July, 1933. Reprinted by permission from *Documents Illustrative of Japan's National Policy* (Nanking: Council of International Affairs, October 27, 1937), pp. 18-31.

the people is gradually sinking to nought. To speak pessimistically, we are simply facing a decadence, a degeneration in the most speedy way and on the largest scale.

2. JAPAN'S OWN FAULT

Let me ask you, having forgotten the great spirit upon which the nation is built, having thrown overboard the very substance and dignity which distinguish the Japanese from other people, what is left here for us Japanese? All the calamities befalling us have crept in through this pitfall. Regarding the fact that Japan has been the object of world contempt and has been insulted by the Chinese, it is after all our fault. As a result of this our fault there arose the Manchurian Incident around which the contending parties rallied back and forth until the League emerged as the center of the whole affair and the whole world besieged Japan. Upon the causes of such a situation we must allow our thoughts to dwell.

The Manchurian Incident did not arise from the trampling of treaties or the encroachment upon sovereign rights, or any such problems. The principal cause is that Japan has been insulted and held contemptuous by the Chinese. That damned League's meddling rights with wrongs is nothing but a proof of its disrespect for Japan. To be slighted by the entire world is precisely the direct cause for Japan's having fallen into this solitary friendless international position. That such is due to Japan's own fault needs, of course, no further explanation, being so self-evident.

The people of Japan must understand the whole argument mentioned above. Japanese people cannot end this present deadlock unless they understand this argument. That the Manchurian Incident has arisen just at this moment is indeed most fortunate, for it is God who, wishing to rouse the Japanese people from their slumber, has been striking the bell of warning. We should never feel pessimistic about this present difficult situation.

Weighing the present international tendency, if we could only stir up the great spirit of the Japanese people, then not only would the international atmosphere change from bad to good but the day when the nations of the world would all bow to us and respect and obey our Imperial Way would also be soon before our eyes. This is something most definite and true regarding which there is not the slightest doubt.

3. THE PRESENT FAR EASTERN CONDITION

The true spirit of our national construction and the Imperial Way which is the crystallization of the great ideal of the Japanese people, considering their nature, should be proclaimed to the end of the Four Seas and developed to the limit of the universe. Hence anything which proves to be an obstacle to their propagation, no matter what it is, should be wiped out with all our might. Concerning this point, it is necessary to examine the present condition of East Asia because the object in the establishment of our constructive plan is to improve our immediate environment. But how is the world of East Asia today?

Our close neighbor China has been shattered by the disturbances during these 20 years and neither has it yet a central government which can claim control of the entire nation, nor does it possess the essentials necessary for a true nation. India has been under the pressure of England, with her three hundred million people trodden and trampled till the whole situation becomes an irretrievable menacing crisis. Or, let us look at the endless fertile land of central Asia and the inexhaustible treasure box of Siberia. Both have been seized now by Russia and enjoy not the slightest freedom. Mongolia the land of peace, has also become a second central Asia. The only country which can yet retain its grace of independence beside our country is the kingdom of Siam. Even this remaining primeval fruit is constantly under menace from its neighbors and can hardly hope for expansion of its power.

Facing such a situation of these various countries of East Asia, Japan, the lord guardian of East Asia by self assumption as well as by universal consent, who is entrusted with the mission to glorify the Imperial Way and to save the multitude, cannot stand by with folded arms and let go her responsibility. Since we are here for righteousness, as Mencius said "when both cannot be possessed at the same time, I sacrifice life to embrace righteousness," so no matter under whatever circumstance we must firmly hold on to our immediate conviction and fight for righteousness.

England is known as a nation of nobility, yet the independence movement (*swaraj* movement) of India has become increasingly feverish year after year. Why? The United States is lauded for its principles of righteousness and humanitarianism, yet carefully analyzing its foreign policy and looking at its activities in Panama, Nicaragua, Cuba, Mexico, and other countries in Central and South

America, what impression do we get? After scrutinizing the civilizations of the various nations in the international arena, we find not even the slightest tinge of our Imperial Way.

The various countries now in East Asia are objects of the white race's oppression. The already awakened Japanese Empire can no longer allow them to tyrannize any more. No matter what nation it is, so long as its movement does not conform to the ideal of the Imperial Way, battle it down. This is the mission of the Japanese Empire according to this definition. We Japanese cannot keep silent in view of calamities or disturbances taking place anywhere in East Asia, for the great ideal of the Japanese Empire is diametrically opposed to the violation of peace. We must have the understanding that even if we should resort to arms, violations of peace and uprisings of a disturbing nature must needs be suppressed by Japan. I believe if we could only cherish this understanding and support it with our force, there would be no need to resort to our inherited precious Sacred Sword before peace could be regulated.

4. THE TRUE MISSION OF THE REIGN OF SHOWA

To keep alive the spirit of the people so fostered and cultivated during the Meiji and the Taisho reigns and to go a step further, to fuse it with the great national construction spirit in order to propagate and glorify the Imperial Way to the end of the four seas, is the true mission of the reign of Showa. The inadequacy of strength is not worth our worry. Why should we worry about that which is material? Everything depends upon our power. With one resolve and at one stroke our object can be accomplished. Whatever that is which obstructs the great plan of the Japanese Empire should be wiped out without the least leniency.

Brethren! Forget the rising storm in East Asia, forget the menacing atmosphere of the entire world? Do not at all be pessimistic? Nor should you be bound by passion and petty obligations and wittingly intoxicate yourselves. Well did Ma Yung say in his Loyalty classic: "Loyalty is not just to uphold your sovereign and forget yourself, to die for your country and forget your families, to be severe in bearing, straight-forward in utterance, and die for a great cause in front of dangers, but to profoundly plan and deeply meditate in order to establish the country and pacify the people."

To establish the country and pacify the people are precisely the effluence of the great spirit of our Empire. You should all the more glorify that one of the three auspicious instruments of killing one person in order to rescue the world, the Sacred Sword, and march toward our great ideal. Look, ah look, glorious and resplendent is the prospect of the reign of Showa.

Chapter 6. An Unprecedented Opportunity

1. JAPAN IS NOT A SHARK

The nations of the world and a part of the Japanese people all consider the Manchurian Incident as having arisen solely out of Japan's desire to seize the rights of Manchuria.

If there is any nation which must have the rights of Manchuria, give them to it, whether it be the United States or Russia. If it really wants to seize them, let it take them. Japan is not an avaricious shark. If Japan is mistaken for a shark, then, first of all, people are doing injustice to the newly arisen people of Manchuria. Japan is a nation which can face both God and man with a clear conscience, that is, a nation which enlightens the world with its Imperial Way.

We want to bring about the bright virtue of the Kingly Way by means of the Imperial Way by first safeguarding the peace of East Asia and then, a step further, establishing upon it the peace of the world. To realize this ideal we use the independence of Manchuria at our starting point. Because of our earnest hope for the peace of the world, there arose the Manchurian Incident; for promoting the welfare of the numberless multitude (mankind), there emerged the independence of Manchukuo. Rights or no rights, it is a very small problem. This point I beg you not to misunderstand.

2. IF IT IS JUST FOR THE PROBLEM OF SUSTENANCE THEN WHAT DIFFICULTY CAN THERE BE?

In present-day society people keep on shouting: "Give us food, give us food!" The shouts shake heaven and earth. If it is simply a question of food, then what difficulty is there? And it does not pay to shout so. Just go to Ginza and Asakusa and beg in front of the cafes and restaurants. Not only will you fill your own stomachs but you will also be able to bring dainty left-overs home for your folks. But this is not the right way. Japanese people, holding the

Imperial Way as their life principle, cannot even dream of such an act. If there is only that which is immediate and practical to consider, then it is easy to tackle the problems of the world. But the people of Japan are definitely not born merely for that which is immediate and practical. The principal of economics today is to increase the ratio of production to its maximum with the least amount of labor and to utilize as much as possible the profits thus secured for self-interest.

This kind of economics does not at all fit the nature of our Japanese people. Japanese people wish to work as much as they can and for the proper amount of production to take proper amount of profit. At night, when there is nothing to do, drink a cup of wine to ease up the drudgery of the day; live in peace at home; and save some money. In case there is more money than necessary, contribute it to society for social affairs and national undertakings. Isn't this a real satisfaction? Indeed true happiness of life lies here! If our people can all cherish this in their bosoms, then there can never be any unemployment nor any injustice. And how can there be any room for Marxism? Because of the immense decrease of labor on the one hand and the irresponsible increase of productive ratio on the other, there arise the problems of unemployment; because people only know how to speculate for themselves, evil thought raises its head.

3. JAPAN IS A HEALTHY STOMACH

Japan, like a large and strong stomach, can digest all, be it Buddhism, Confucianism, or whatever it is, because the spirit of Japan is free and powerful, not at all static but all assimilating. Moreover, it can Nipponize its object. This is a point which the Japanese people should be proud of.

Language for example. The Chinese people created with great effort the Chinese language, which the Japanese people borrowed, adding to it their own invention of the 51 radicals and using the Chinese language as a progressive tool, while in China, that country's own language became static and China herself has been bound by it ever since. Civilized as the Chinese people are today, they have to encounter a certain amount of language difficulty even in sending a telegram. Thus compared with China, Japan is at least a thousand years ahead. Since the Meiji Reformation, European civilization has been imported and half of it has been digested while the other half has been swallowed. Those people who have failed to digest it are not true Japanese, they are no more than deserters from the unswerving path of the Japanese and they have forgotten the glory of Japan.

Every true Japanese cannot be other than free and possess a strong elastic digestive organ; he cannot do other than possess the Japanese spirit, which shines high above all nations and is capable of engendering the greatest assimilating power to absorb everything.

4. WHAT IS THE USE OF THE LEAGUE!

Look at our diplomatic history, which is but a condensed picture of our yielding submissive diplomacy. The treaties signed immediately before or after the Meiji Reformation amount to no more than submissive agreements to whatever other nations have dictated. Let us forget that. The three-power intervention before and after the Sino-Japanese War was an instance of this. Japan simply can neither cry nor laugh but just say "yes" and "yes." Even this insult by China in trampling down all of the treaties signed we can let go. But with regard to the action of the disarmament conference in limiting Japan's ratio to three against the five of England and the five of America, that is indeed most unbearable.

At present, in dealing with the Manchurian question, no matter how the League exercises its power and how the Nine-Power Treaty is applied to Japan, Japan maintains the same attitude throughout. For the peace of the Far East and for the peace of the world, Manchukuo should be independent. And we dare to speak out. Let me ask you then, what is the use of the League of Nations? What is the use of the Nine-Power Treaty? Is it not that the League of Nations is known as the organization for promoting world peace? Is it not that for the peace of the Far East the Nine-Power Treaty was signed? If the League is just working for the benefit of Europe and America, then, thanks, we don't want it any more. If the Nine-Power Treaty is working just for the self-interest of the nations concerned then let them not open their mouths.

5. JAPANESE PEOPLE SHOULD EXAMINE THEMSELVES

However for one thing there are different views. Since the nations of the world are centering their attention upon the moves of our country, it is precisely the right moment for us to extend our Imperial Way. Let the world know that the great latent power of our Japanese people is evident today. This is indeed an unprecedented opportunity! At the most critical moment Japanese people cannot but first examine themselves; that is, first eliminate those people who can only swallow the imported western civilization. We must lead these strays as no other than off-springs of this kind of education. From now on we Japanese cannot but turn back to teach the Europeans and Americans. Anyhow, this is no longer the time for importations from Europe and America but exportations from Japan.

Let us take this Manchurian Incident as an opportunity to make manifest to the world the real power of Japan. Let us propagate the great true virtue of our imperial country in order to establish the three great united states of Europe, America and Asia. Not until then can we talk about the peace of the world.

Chapter 9. The Awakening of the Japanese People

1. RESOLVE OF THE PEOPLE

It is now one year since the army of the great Nippon Empire, on the land of Manchuria, wielded the auspicious sword of our Empire. During this one year, while the dead bodies of our soldiers lie yet unburied in the North and the blood of our men besmears the mud south of the Yangtze River, the officers and soldiers, one and all, fought without ceasing. For the enthusiasm and unwavering support of the multitude at home which had instigated the fighting spirit of these patriotic soldiers who sacrificed themselves in order to accomplish this great deed, we Japanese people, looking back at the victory of this one year cannot but shed our tears in gratitude. However, how can this great valor of our people and their precious spirit of sacrifice score the final victory? This of course depends upon whether we have really become awakened now or not. Now in Manchuria, out of the natural consequence of the Manchurian Incident and through the cooperative efforts of Japan and Manchukuo, there has newly emerged a virtuous nation. Our Imperial Empire, assuming the mission granted by Heaven, does not hesitate nor hold back lending assistance, both spiritual and material, or from giving whatever support may be necessary to the new nation of Manchuria, and it is deeply concerned with the latter's well-being. Since things are as they are, whether people like it or not, let us pay no attention to them. I firmly believe that this is a development in the history of Far Eastern politics which is a great duty and responsibility put upon us Japanese by Heaven.

Yet the Far East, which now has the Sino-Japanese controversy as the center of its political world, has lost its true significance whether in dealing with that which is domestic or international, spiritual or material. Of course many causes are working behind the scenes, yet, considering them all together, the loss is due entirely to our lack of self-realization, our inability to understand the divine mission of our great Nippon race, and to the fact that the pure, noble, and lofty Japanese mind has been darkened by the clouds of Western utilitarianism. Consequently we lose the enthusiasm and courage so characteristic of the members of our race, who are guardians of the peace in the Far East and creators of new civilization.

Since we have come upon this blind alley, we cannot but make a clear cut resolve by calling back our new life, and, wielding our auspicious sword, we should march forward. This represents the true nature of the Manchurian Incident and the Shanghai hostilities. When we open our eyes and look into the distance, we find the present situation as follows:

(a) Concerning the creation of a new civilization, upon which the existence of mankind depends, there is a natural manifestation of the development and progress of the fusion of the civilizations East and West;

(b) The Japanese race must all once more truly understand their divine mission, together with the necessary predicaments, sufferance and great difficulties which they have to encounter.

Since things are as they are, whether people can handle this trying situation or not is of no concern to us. Just see whether the Imperial Empire can really become the great Japan and a balancing power in the world like the other powers or will remain forever a small Japan huddling over a few islands in the Far East, with its power stretching no farther than its own boundary within the confines of the Pacific. This is indeed a great problem. No matter to which direction you turn, the solution of it all depends upon our understanding of the real situation of the Far East and the resolve of our nationals.

Confronted with such a great and different situation, and for the permanent establishment of our nation and our race, should we assume the role of self-determination we could not but take into consideration beforehand the fact that all kinds of obstacles and obstructing forces will befall us within the country and without.

2. THE STRUGGLE OF OUR NATIONALS

Just take into consideration the recognition of Manchukuo. Since the League of Nations is as such and with the existence of England, America, France and nations which assume an air of superiority together with their designs, which are adopted purely for the utilitarian reasons, not only is it a fact that their designs cannot conform to our policy but these designs also hinder its progress. Being thus forced to our limit, we must think beforehand of decisively making our great national resolve.

Also, with regard to the pacification designs of our Imperial Empire, from now on we cannot but spend many lives and large sums of money for its sacrifice. Carefully study the present psychology of our nationals; if we are to accomplish this goal, much greater efforts must be made. I firmly believe that the only way to wipe out the obstacles and hindrances within and without in order to lead our nation to the realm of glory is to be aware of the existence of such obstacles and hindrances, to be alert and to struggle, every one of us in the Empire, to the end.

That affairs have developed most favorably to the present stage is due to the divine sovereignty of our heavenly Emperor and therefore they cannot be otherwise. Nevertheless, no less significant is the fact that a group of sagacious men, with their sense of self-sacrifice, their dauntless courage and determination, have fought for the cause of righteousness and their noble spirit and deeds have inspired the entire race to the same spirit newly awakened but latent in them.

For this reason we soldiers should be the more resolved to be the potent elements in supporting and upholding the imperial plan and in expanding our national power. We must obey His Majesty's imperial order. Our conduct must be pure and upright, our steps proper and glorious, thus seeking to strengthen the conviction of our nationals as the pivoting force of our race-mission within and without and causing nations of the world to respect the greatness and dignity of our imperial army. Brave and dauntless, we proceed now to definitely establish the foundation of our national task.

Anyway, the Empire's design for the continent is not a temporary and local affair but a lasting undertaking as vital as the very existence of the Empire itself. From now on, in the few years to come, the Far Eastern political situation, having the Manchurian question as its center, will be, I fear, full of unrest, each year worse than the preceding one. Consequently, the people of Japan, in dealing with the matter, should be all the more firmly resolved, facing the facts in the most practical way and developing, expanding as far as possible. Should there be any laxity, then all the accomplishments so far achieved would turn to nought.

In 1914 Germany lost the victory which she had won in 1870. The great conquest and ambitious designs of our continental expansion established by the Empire in early Japanese history met a serious setback at the battle of Po Chiang Chun (A.D. 663). We Japanese people should take it as a mirror of warning.*

Our affairs today depend entirely upon the determination and effort of every one of us. Should we be so resolved and struggle hard, then complete victory will be ours. Our forefathers, in the battle with the forces of Kubla Khan (1274) as well as during the Meiji Reformation (1867-73) and the Sino-Japanese and Russo-Japanese wars, made unceasing and numberless sacrifices and encountered many dangers and difficulties before they were able to bequeath to us this our present Empire.

In our veins is injected the noblest blood of sacrifice going back for 2,600 years. Whether Japan is to become a great empire or not all depends upon the awakening and struggle of our people.

Chapter 10. The True Mission of the Japanese Race

1. IN THE BODIES OF THE JAPANESE PEOPLE IS THE JAPANESE SPIRIT

Having encountered this momentous situation, to gather together and actually pull out our swords and end the deadlock is of course a happiness. But turn back our glance and see what regrets there are—do you not see that there are too many people without the spirit, the soul? Do you not see that there are too many mechanical slaves, machine builders? Is it not that as a result of this lack of soul we have fallen into this present difficult situation?

---

* General Araki refers here to the crushing defeat the Japanese sustained at the hands of the Chinese general Liu Jen-kwei of the T'ang Dynasty which ended the Japanese aggression on the continent during the early part of Japanese history. Po Chiang Chun is on the western coast of South Korea.

3. THE MISSION OF THE JAPANESE *

Europe recognizes only Europe as the world. The one which contends with Europe in settling world disputes is America (the United States). Under the banner of the Monroe Doctrine, the Americans settle American disputes themselves, heedless of any European interference. For this reason the world only knows about Europe and America and does not know of Asia. And so, despite all her conquests and accomplishments, they do not recognize Japan nor have they confidence in her. Since things have come to the present stage, we Japanese people must have the spirit and power to convince the entire world of Europe and America of the true spirit of Asia, the civilization of Asia, the benevolence of Asia, and going a step further, make manifest to them the mission of Japan. Let the people of Europe and America recognize, let the whole world recognize, that Japan is here and now shouldering the whole responsibility of Asia. If we do not possess even this strength and conviction, then do we deserve to be called the Great Japan of Asia in the Far East? Last year in the League of Nations we battled alone against 13 nations. This time we might have to fight single-handed against 56 of them. No matter what she is to the entire world, since the present condition in Asia is as such, and for the protection of the peace in Asia as well as for the welfare of the whole Asiatic race, Japan, vanguard of the Asiatic battle front, must uphold our imperial house, which lives and dies, rises and falls, with its supreme principle of justice and mercy, which, extending to the corners of the four seas, will stand as does humanity, and, meeting the test of the ages to come, will be embraced by all without hesitation. Should there be any one here thwarting this our undertaking, no matter who he is, he should by all means be pushed aside. And in order to let Europe and America know of this our spirit we must act in the same way as the first manifestation of our soul in dealing with the Manchurian question today.

5. WE SHOULD HOLD FIRM TO OUR CONVICTION †

The present time is a moment of strife within and without. We must obey our Japanese "way," maintain the same attitude in assisting to realize the imperial plan, and promote the welfare of the

* No. 2 is omitted.

† No. 4 is omitted.

multitude in order to be loyal to His Majesty our Heavenly Emperor. It is only right to proceed upon the road of self-reliance with this intention, and whatever we do and whatever we get in such a way will be no other than the good fortune of the multitude. I earnestly hope that you all will cherish to be loyal to His Majesty our Heavenly Emperor and march forward fighting without surcease.

To go after that which is selfish and indulge in the passions is something which cannot be done at this moment of national and international crisis. Every move must be taken according to the dictate of our national conviction. By our national conviction is meant the great ideal of righteousness; to ourselves, it is the everlasting peace of the East.

Reference Notes

Chapter I

1. Hiro-o Sassa, "Our Public Opinion: Voices Heard and Unheard," *Contemporary Japan*, March, 1937, Vol. V, No. 4, pp. 549, 551.
2. F. Brinkley and Baron Kikuchi, *History of the Japanese People* (New York: Encyclopaedia Britannica Co., 1915), p. 286.
3. Uichi Iwasaki, *Working Forces in Japanese Politics* (New York: Columbia University, 1921), pp. 64, 65.
4. Basil Hall Chamberlain, *The Invention of a New Religion* (London: Watts & Co., 1912), pp. 13-14.
5. Alfred Stead, *Great Japan* (London: 1906), p. 38, as quoted by M. Frederick Nelson, "Feudalistic Propaganda in Modern Japan," *Amerasia*, November, 1938, p. 450.
6. *Ibid.*, pp. 57-58.
7. D. C. Holtom, *The National Faith of Japan* (New York: E. P. Dutton & Co., 1938), p. 315.

Chapter II

1. Yoshi S. Kuno, *Japanese Expansion on the Asiatic Continent* (Berkeley, Cal.: University of California Press, 1937), Vol. I, p. 30.
2. Chikao Fujisawa, *Japanese and Oriental Political Philosophy* (Tokyo: Research Dept. of the Daito-Bunka-Kyokai [Great Oriental Culture Society], 1935), pp. 247, 249.
3. See Hu Shih, *Historical Foundations for a Democratic China*, reprinted from Edmund J. James lectures on government, University of Illinois, 1941, p. 4.
4. Karl Robert Reischauer, *Japan: Government—Politics* (New York: Thos. Nelson & Sons, 1939), p. 36.

5. E. M. Satow, "The Revival of Pure Shin-tau," *Transactions of the Asiatic Society of Japan*, Vol. III, Part I, October 14-December 23, 1874. Appendix, p. 27.
6. Yutaka Hibino, *Nippon Shindo Ron*, or *The National Ideals of the Japanese People* (London: Cambridge University Press, 1928), pp. 18-19. According to Professor Charles S. Braden (*Amerasia*, May, 1938, p. 149) this work "is widely used as a textbook in the Middle Schools in Japan, has gone through several editions and is said by its translator to represent genuinely the thought of the Japanese people."
7. Uichi Iwasaki, *op. cit.*, p. 64.
8. Reischauer, *op. cit.*, p. 73.
9. B. H. Chamberlain, *op. cit.*, p. 16.
10. Chikao Fujisawa, *op. cit.*, pp. 80-1.

Chapter III

1. Yosoburo Takekoshi, *Economic Aspects of the History of the Civilization of Japan* (London: George Allen & Unwin, 1930), Vol. I, pp. 342 ff. This three-volume work contains a great deal of useful information with regard to early Japanese expansion.
2. *Ibid.*, pp. 339-40.
3. *Ibid.*, p. 451 ff.
4. Kuno, *op. cit.*, Vol. I, p. 308.
5. Letter of January 1, 1617, to the East India Company, quoted by M. D. Kennedy, *The Problem of Japan* (London: Nisbet & Co., 1939), pp. 38-39.
6. Kuno, *op. cit.*, pp. 61, 62.
7. Takekoshi, *op. cit.*, Vol. I, pp. 490 ff.
8. James Murdoch, *A History of Japan* (Yokohama: Kelly and Walsh, 1903), Vol. II, p. 305.
9. Kuno, *op. cit.*, Vol. I, p. 143.
10. Murdoch, *op. cit.*, Vol. II, pp. 305-6.
11. *Ibid.*, p. 304.
12. Takekoshi, *op. cit.*, Vol. I, pp. 477-8.

Chapter IV

1. Kuno, *op. cit.*, Vol. II, p. 23.
2. *Ibid.*, pp. 96-7.

3. *Ibid.*, p. 64.
4. Murdoch, *op. cit.*, Vol. I, p. 11.
5. W. G. Aston, *A History of Japanese Literature* (New York: D. Appleton-Century Co., Inc., 1937), pp. 325-6. This appears to be a summing-up of Motoori's attitude rather than a literal translation.
6. Satow, *op. cit.*, p. 24.
7. *Ibid.*, p. 58.
8. *Ibid.*, p. 52.
9. Robert Louis Stevenson, *Familiar Studies of Men and Books.*
10. Iichiro Tokutomi, "Life of Shoin Yoshida," translated from the Japanese by Horace E. Coleman, *Transactions of the Asiatic Society of Japan*, Vol. XLV, Part 1, 1917.
11. *Ibid.*, p. 163.
12. Francis L. Hawks, *Narrative of the Expedition of an American Squadron to the China Seas and Japan* (New York: D. Appleton and Company, 1856), p. 487.
13. Kengi Hamada, *Prince Ito* (Tokyo: Sanseido Co., 1936), p. 14.
14. *Ibid.*, p. 16.
15. *Ibid.*, p. 46.
16. Rikitaro Fujisawa, *The Recent Aims and Political Development of Japan* (New Haven: Yale University Press, 1923), pp. 31-2.
17. Tokutomi, *op. cit.*, p. 105.
18. *Ibid.*, p. 161.
19. *Ibid.*, p. 162.
20. Izuru Shimmura, *Western Influences on Japanese History and Culture in Earlier Periods (1540-1860)* (Tokyo: Kokusai Bunka Shinkokai, 1936), pp. 18 ff.

Chapter V

1. Tatsuo Kawai, *The Goal of Japanese Expansion* (Tokyo: The Hokkuseido Press, 1938), pp. 68 ff.
2. Tokutomi, *op. cit.*, p. 143.
3. *Ibid.*, p. 159.
4. *Documents Illustrative of Japan's National Policy* (Nanking: Council of International Affairs, October 27, 1937), pp. 45-58.

5. Lieut.-General Kenji Doihara, "Roots of Japan's National Policy Toward China," *Amerasia*, March, 1939, p. 21.
6. Quoted by Dr. Charles Iglehart in *Japan Christian Yearbook* for 1941.
7. Quoted by Dr. Charles Iglehart in *Japan Christian Yearbook* for 1941.
8. Mousheng Hsitien Lin, "Paranoia Nipponica," *T'ien Hsia Monthly*, October, 1939, Vol. IX, No. 3.
9. Raymond Leslie Buell, *Japanese Immigration* (Boston: World Peace Foundation, 1924), pp. 314-15.
10. Masaharu Anesaki, *Religious Life of the Japanese People* (Tokyo: Kokusai Bunka Shinkokai, 1938), p. 102.

Chapter VI

1. Alvin Johnson, New School for Social Research *Bulletin*, No. 6, New York, December 8, 1941.
2. *Economic Survey of the Pacific Area* (New York: International Secretariat, Institute of Pacific Relations, 1941), Table 21, p. 31.
3. E. F. Penrose, *Population Theories and Their Application with Special Reference to Japan* (Food Research Institute, Stanford University, Cal., 1934), pp. 98-99.
4. Shiroshi Nasu, *Aspects of Japanese Agriculture* (New York: Institute of Pacific Relations, 1941), p. 3.
5. Karl J. Pelzer, *Economic Survey of the Pacific Area*, Part 1, "Population and Land Utilization," p. 31.
6. Guenther Stein, *Made in Japan* (London: Methuen & Co., 1935), p. 162.
7. *Ibid.*, p. 202.
8. *Problems of the Pacific, 1936* (New York: Institute of Pacific Relations), p. 64.
9. Miriam S. Farley, *The Problem of Japanese Trade Expansion in the Post-War Situation* (New York: International Secretariat, Institute of Pacific Relations, 1940), pp. 43-44, 61.
10. *Ibid.*, pp. 75 ff. Also see *Economic Handbook of the Pacific Area* (New York: Doubleday, Doran & Co., 1934), pp. 587 ff.
11. *The Industrialization of Japan and Manchukuo 1930-1940.* Edited by E. B. Schumpeter (contributors G. C. Allen, M. S.

Gordon, E. F. Penrose, E. B. Schumpeter). (New York: The Macmillan Company, 1940), p. 11.

12. G. C. Allen, *Japanese Industry: Its Recent Development and Present Condition* (New York: Institute of Pacific Relations, 1940).
13. Roswell G. Townsend, "Is There a Japanese Population Problem?" *Amerasia*, May, 1939, p. 138.
14. Westel W. Willoughby, *Japan's Case Examined* (Baltimore: The Johns Hopkins Press, 1940), p. 117.
15. In a lecture before the Japan Society, London, on March 28, 1929, reported in *Transactions of the Japan Society*, London, 1929, pp. 110 ff.
16. Julean Arnold, "China's Fate and America's Future," *Amerasia*, June, 1939, p. 169.

Chapter VII

1. Sir George Sansom, "Liberalism in Japan," *Foreign Affairs*, April, 1941, p. 552.
2. Shunji Toyama, "The Tyranny of the Living and the Dead," *Amerasia*, April, 1941, pp. 80, 82.
3. Toshio Shiratori, "Fascism Versus the Popular Front," *Contemporary Japan*, March, 1938, Vol. VI, pp. 582 ff.
4. *Amerasia*, October, 1940, pp. 365 ff.
5. Quoted in *The Spectator*, London, November 17, 1939.
6. Translation by Mr. Jen Tai from Mr. Liu Wen-Tao's Chinese version as published in the *Ta Kung Pao*, May-July, 1933, included in *Documents Illustrative of Japan's National Policy* (Nanking: Council of International Affairs, October 27, 1937), Vol. V, Nos. 1 and 2.
7. Chikao Fujisawa, *op. cit.*, pp. 230, 256, 263, 276, 284.
8. *Far East Crisis*, reprint of articles published in *The Times* (London: Times Publishing Company, 1941), pp. 9-10.
9. Sir Robert Vansittart, *Black Record* (London: Hamish Hamilton, 1941), p. 49.
10. Kenneth W. Colegrove, *Militarism in Japan* (Boston: World Peace Foundation, 1936), pp. 52-3.
11. Tatsuo Kawai, *op. cit.*, pp. 93-4.
12. See Kenneth W. Colegrove, "The New Order in East Asia," *Far Eastern Quarterly*, November, 1941, Vol. I, No. 1, p. 23.

13. Wilfrid Fleisher, *Volcanic Isle* (New York: Doubleday, Doran & Company, Inc., 1941), pp. 190-1.

CHAPTER VIII

1. Vansittart, *op. cit.*, p. 15.
2. W. W. McLaren, author of *A Political History of Japan*, in a review entitled "The Political Development of Japan," *Transactions of the Asiatic Society of Japan*, November, 1914.
3. Freda Utley, *Japan's Feet of Clay* (New York: W. W. Norton & Company, Inc., 1937), p. 27.
4. Wilfrid Fleisher, *op. cit.*, p. 331.
5. Sir George Sansom, *op. cit.*, p. 560.
6. Nathaniel Peffer, "Fatalism—Their Strength, Their Weakness," *New York Times Magazine*, December 14, 1941, p. 7.
7. Massaharu Aneskia, *The Religious Life of the Japanese People* (Tokyo: Kokusai Bunka Shinkokai, 1938), p. 102.
8. Vansittart, *op. cit.*, p. 18.
9. See *Voice of China* release, November 29, 1941.

Index